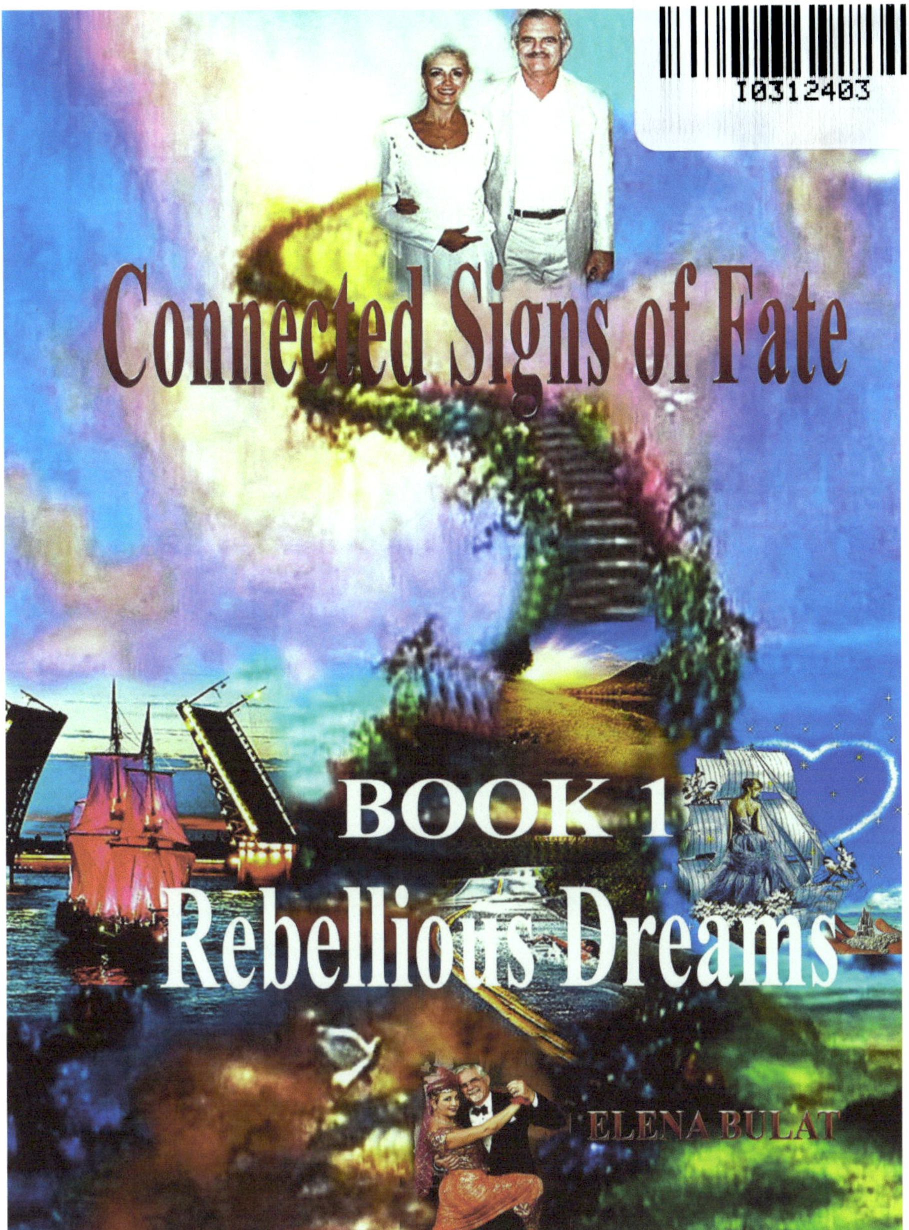

Connected Signs of Fate

Book 1

Rebellious Dreams

Elena Bulat

Disclaimer

"This book reflects the author's present recollections of experiences over time. Some names and characteristics have been changed, some events have been compressed, and some dialogue has been recreated.

Space and time have been rearranged to suit the convenience of the book, and with the exception of public figures, any resemblance to persons living or dead is coincidental. The opinions expressed are those of the characters and should not be confused with the author's.

The text, characters and plot of this book could take place anywhere in the world. The book does not describe specific individuals. It cannot be used against anybody or in the court of law. It is only a creation of the writer."

***

Every movement is a dance of life, if you decide to move.
Love your only Life
The Walking One Will Overpower the Road...

***

Contents

About the Trilogy	5
Bright Light	6
Discovery	9
Greeks	11
Father	12
First Days	13
Abandoned	16
Once Upon a Time	18
Broken Trust	19
Escape	20
Secrets	23
Relatives	24
Pearls	27
Lost Treasure	29
Broken Promises	31
Looses	33
Binding Threads	35
Berlin Prison	38
Alena's Arrest	44
Complain	52
Punishment	54
Leningrad	64
Artist Valery	65
Crossroads	66
Paris	72
Visa	76

***

About the Trilogy

This is a trilogy about the strange signs of fate. Two people on the different continent experienced amazing coincidences of their life events at the same age, including the Soviet prison and Berlin prison. Finally, their similar views on life and the same vision of their happiness united two heroes, who lived on opposite parts of the earth.

Invisible, connecting threads sped to the other end of the earth, across the ocean, continuing to weave the paths of fate, connecting the past with the future. The whirlwinds of fate weaved the lives of a Soviet woman Alena and American man Victusha. Those invisible threads connected impossible destinies together.

The trilogy tells about a girl Alena who dreamed to live a beautiful life and one day she moved to America. This is a story about her life under different circumstances and conditions. Miraculous transformations came to Alena with her belief in the happiness, which filled her soul with joy, giving the same joy to her man.

The trilogy "Connected Signs of Fate" has 3 books. Book 1. Rebellious Dreams. Book 2. Average Bean. Book 3. Ring of a Carousel. Enjoy your time and be inspired.

Bright Light

During the first nine months of her new life, Alena lay in a very comfortable place, curled up and hiding. It was the most warm, soft and safe place in the world. In addition, this was the only serene, peaceful time of pleasures, when there was no need to think about anything material at all. Sometimes, from somewhere above, wise knowledge and great ideas of the past generations seemed to seep into Alena mind. Then she bounced in amazement, bumping lightly against the soft walls of her first home. Even before she was born, she knew something very important about the world, clearly saw what it was filled with, and why she was going into it. But with each passing month, the space around her became smaller, bringing a sense of anxiety from a closed tightness. Once this feeling of claustrophobia became so unbearable that it was necessary to find a way out. Finally she made up her mind and courageously began to climb forward.

There was a dark and wet tunnel on her way, and a ray of light at the end of it shone, and beckoned with hope, promising joy. After hours of tiring travel, this welcome light finally approached. Alena emerged with her eyes wide open, anticipating happiness. But, suddenly, a short and painful slap met her, instead of a joyful greeting. Along with the "medical slap" in the first second of appearing on this planet, Alena immediately forgot all the wisdom of the past generations. The huge knowledge about the World and the Universe that she received there, behind, in her first house instantly evaporated somewhere. The blow of a hard hand like a magic wand completely erased all the information. But still, for a long time, then there was a strange feeling in her that she knew something enchanting and special. But this well of knowledge seemed was lost forever.

Suddenly Alena found herself in an empty room with a white ceiling and green walls covered with oil paint. From a sharp cold, an unpleasant slap and resentment, and just to, at least, somehow express her disagreement with such an unfriendly greeting, she began to scream loudly, jerking thin legs without muscles and long twisted arms. She called at least someone for help, hoping for care and love. An unsmiling nurse walked in and tightly wrapped the child in a rag, tightly pulling the ends together. The helpless Alena was not able to even lift a finger. She was used to complete freedom in her past comfortable home. It seemed unfair to be held captive by someone else's will. And even more despair swept Alena from this violence and her forced captivity. Unable to do anything, for some time she continued to shout loudly about the lawlessness of the new "arrivals" and the injustice of such treatment. But then she was tired and fell asleep, deciding to find out later all the circumstances and reasons for this not so hospitable meeting.

On the night of Alena's birth, a winter hurricane roared outside the window, drizzled with thorny rain and snow. The strong Northeast wind - Nord-Ost - buzzed in the electro wires, recently appeared in the town, tearing out the new posts and centuries-old trees. On that stormy January night, Alena's uncle, Reanold, tried to get to Gelendzhik, led by his love for his twenty-eight-year-old sister. He wanted to support her in delivering to the Earth such a valuable gift - a new Person. But due to a severe storm, he was stuck at the Novorossiysk railway station, forty kilometers away. No one undertook to steer through the mountains along the steep, winding and narrow road, risking their lives in such darkness and storm. Thus, on this unforgettable, significant night, mother Emma remained in the hospital alone, successfully coping with her difficult, but noble work.

When Alena woke up again, she saw a round ball in front of her nose. A delicious smell emanated from it. But, just in case, Alena turned away in the other direction. What if this is a new trap? But someone stubbornly directed this soft, fragrant ball into her mouth. Alena twisted her head, worried also by the fact that it might not fit inside. And milk splashed into her face. Then this pink ball was still surprisingly easily pushed inside her mouth, and she almost choked on a huge amount of sweet drink. There was so much milk that she was forced to swallow it quickly so as not to choke. However, after a minute she successfully mastered it, and the stream of this warm rain became pleasant and soothing to her. In addition, some very gentle voice whispered: *"Sleep my baby, your mother is nearby, and a beautiful world awaits you ahead."*

After eating and a lulling voice, Alena felt much better and even a little more confident. She wholeheartedly believed this quiet and loving voice. All these new efforts and excitements plunged her into a long, sound sleep. She dreamed of a joyful and happy life. Her appearance on Earth began with an unexpected slap, but after the first humiliation came the hope and comfort brought by her mother's warm, soothing milk.

So the day passed, and then the second, but no one came to visit them. Alena did not feel anymore the tenderness of her mother, and her caring voice no longer sounded for her. Mom was upset, her milk became bitter. Alena refused to drink it, and cried.

***

Only a few months passed, but Alena acutely felt everything and understood the deep essence of things. It often happened that no one was near her little, painted in lettuce-colored metal crib. There was no one to just shake, talk, or fall in love with a little girl. Even when she wanted to use the toilet, no one came, and lying in her wet and dirty linen was unpleasant. And then, Alena again cried from hopeless despair. Unable to speak and call for the help, she simply screamed because of her helplessness, feeling her loneliness more and more.

In a small resort town on the Black Sea, in the ancient Greek settlement with the strange name Gelendzhik ("White Bride"), a new Guest of the Earth appeared - Alena. On a stormy winter night, her first trip to this planet, her first voyage to life, finally took place.

Later, Alena felt that she was very different from the others. In addition, her grandmother, in whose house she was brought up, always emphasized that Alena was a very special girl. All this reinforced her sense of uniqueness. Alena lived as if in a dream, understanding people and animals without words. She was watching what was happening around her, as if from the side. This strange feeling of a "wanderer and an unexpected alien" was always nearby, during all periods of her life. Miraculous transformations came to Alena with her faith in future happiness, and filled her soul with joy. So her miracles in the riddle began. Up down. Believe and wait.

***

Discovery

Gelendzhik is a city of dreams on the Black sea. People meet in the magical twilight of sunset. The music of the sea breaks into fate, a whirlwind of dance circles, creating new lives. Love lives in the musical passages of the old city. There appeared the life of Alena. The life of her mother, her friends and enemies remained forever there. Fate made a full circle, and once dipped Alena into the fire of unsolved secrets and passions. Once she suddenly found on the Internet old photographs, relics of her heroic grandfather. They had been stolen from his house, and only a bundle of photo paper from the first day of the war, dated June 22, 1941 remained to his relatives. Those photos returned Alena to her childhood, and she began to write her books.

***

Childhood. Amid the hustle and bustle of the day, we have no time to drop by. Only sometimes at night do we open the curtains of memory and wander again in the half-forgotten mazes of painfully bitter or sweet memories of the past. In order to protect a person from too painful memory, nature has created a special protective mechanism, blocking stresses or tragic events of the past. So for a long time Alena did not want to look back into this well of early memory. It was impossible to feel the sharp pain of her childhood losses again. But somehow, on a cruise ship in the Pacific Ocean, multi-colored cubes twisted emotional memory, and suddenly transferred her back to the first months of her life on the Earth. She suddenly remembered a lot of what was hidden behind a heavy curtain.

The future of each child is determined by the way his parents, and especially the mother, treat him in early childhood. When Alena was not even a year old she experienced several heavy emotional blows. Her young mother, Emma, who fought for her honor and independence, was forced to leave her tiny daughter in her grandmother's house, and to go to work in Sakhalin.

Emma was a Russian natural blonde beauty, with beautiful blue eyes looking at the world with the hope of love and fidelity. But from her youth she worked very hard. It never occurred to her to use makeup, do hairstyles, or go for a massage. Alena never saw her caring for herself at all. Therefore, she was very pleased when her mother twice a year, before the big holidays, was dyeing her eyebrows with makeup. Then she looked especially fresh, and at home everyone became joyful.

Emma was the eldest and very obedient daughter. She helped her mother in everything, nursed two younger brothers, and meekly carried the burdens and deprivations of a nomadic life on her shoulders. Her father Minai was military, and by nature cruel and sarcastic. He often laughed at his daughter and criticized her for any oversights. There was no love, no peace, and no comfort in the family. Already under the bombing, under the onslaught of the Nazi troops, the family barely escaped from Izhevsk. Shortly after the war, her parents and their many relatives moved to Gelendzhik, to the sleepy little place, far from all troubles. During the war, the military accumulated quite a lot of money. Emma's father, Minai, and his brothers were able to buy quite large pieces of land with small houses. At that time, Emma went to college to study to be an accountant, and reunited with them later.

***

Greeks

The stunning resort town by the sea almost year-round was filled by half-naked and very accessible beauties, shamelessly walking along the embankments. They came from all over the Soviet Union not only for recreation, but mainly for new adventures and romance. In a magical town it was impossible to find faithful husbands devoted to their wives. The sea air of the town, saturated with Pitsunda pine, was dizzy to both local residents and vacationers.

The fragrance was especially magnificent in May 1953. The exciting smell of apricot and cherry trees, acacia, lilac and roses drove everyone crazy from awakening passions. In the town, all the men were crazy about the recently arrived beauty Emma. That year, she was often dancing tango in the Primorye Recreation Center, and fell in love with Konstantin Arfanov, the future father of Alena.

Alena's Greek grandfather was also a cheerful handsome man, and was known as a prosperous merchant. He had vineyards near Gelendzik, in Praskoveevka. He often hired assistants to harvest the grapes, and several local families took care of his land and business. But as a result of denunciations by envious persons he, with a group of other successful Greeks, was sentenced to be shot without a trial. He had only one fault was that he was Greek.

The situation of Soviet power after the revolution and the Civil War was precarious. The restoration of the monarchy in Greece in 1935 was also dangerous for the Soviet Union. Among other events of the "Greek" operation, all national Greek schools, publishing houses, and newspapers in the USSR were closed. Other Greeks of the Soviet Black Sea coast were deported to Siberia and the Kazakhstan in freight wagons. Their property was transferred to others in the population. During the "Great Terror" (1937-1938) about 15 thousand Greeks (Soviet and Greek citizens) were arrested.

Stalin (Yezhov, a Soviet secret police official) signed a Declaration which clearly indicated the number of Greeks who needed to be arrested and how many of them would be shot or sent to camps for 10 years. Only three days were allotted for the preparation of lists with surnames for the issuance of arrest warrants.

***

Father

As recalled the grandmother of Konstantin, Greek Maria, the boy was then only ten years old. He was terribly shocked about the execution and funeral of his father, also Constantine. These tragic events put an indelible mark on both the child and his entire family.

Many years later, trying to find out at least something about the past of her relatives, Alena found on the Internet "Protocol No. 126 of September 5, 1938", where under the number 11 was the name of her Greek grandfather. So, this is how she for the first time suddenly found out about her grandfather: *"No. 11. Arfanov Konstantin Georgievich (born in 1906), a citizen of the USSR, place of birth - the village of Praskoveevka, Gelendzhik district, Krasnodar Territory. Sentence - Shoot. "*

The mother of little Konstantin, Elena Arfanova, lived near Emma's house. She worked as a teacher in school number 3, where Alena later studied. From the whisper of her relatives, Alena learned that Elena Savvichna was able to convince someone in the registry office to correct several letters in their surname in order to avoid subsequent repressions. As the son of an "executed enemy of the people," the boy Konstantin (like Alena later), grew up surrounded by constant secrets and terrified whispers behind him. This produced a feeling of distrust in him and about everything around him. From childhood, he experienced a sense of fear and anxiety, and new people and a sharp change of scenery were a source of stress.

While growing up, Konstantin was not indifferent to spectacular, vibrant women. He was constantly looking for the love and affection that he lacked from childhood. Konstantin made every effort to attract the attention of the twenty-seven-year-old beauty Emma. They were close in the spring and summer of 1953. Then, Konstantin began strongly to ogle and fool around with other women. He, like other local guys, was looking for entertainment with easily accessible vacationers, and spent most of his time with them. Emma and Konstantin did not get married, as he promised. Emma could not forgive the betrayal of her lover. But the saddest thing was that she could never get rid or forget her bitter past. Konstantin always lived nearby, over the fence, in his comfortable house.

Once, even before the complete break, when Alena was several months old, Konstantin and Emma took a joint photograph. The girl was sitting in her mother's arms. And her father held her hand. All her life Alena remembered her father's striped shirt from that photo. After parting, from the resentment and wanting to erase the painful memory of her first lover, Emma tore his face from all of the few photos that they took together. All her childhood, Alena terribly missed her father and even sometimes saw him in a dream.

***

First Days

The first months, Alena and her mother eke out a miserable existence in an old, disheveled shack on the corner of Shevchenko and Sovetskaya, five blocks from Emma's parents' house. This shack with a tiny piece of land Konstantin's grandmother, taking pity on single mother Emma, gave her for very little money.

The shack where Emma lived with her daughter Alena had only one room, a low entrance, and a creaky door. The earthen floor was in some places covered with rotten boards. And on the windows, according to the old custom, wooden sashes hung for security. They could be closed at night only by hand, going outside. Around Emma's house was a small garden. And at the father's fence stood a huge tree, cut half by a shell fragment.

One old women said that a bomb fell in the garden when the Nazis bombed the port of Novorossiysk, forty kilometers from Gelendzhik. The house was wrenched from the blast, and it was dangerous to live in. Alena was afraid, listening to the stories about shells that flew near their house and put everyone in mortal danger. And she thought it was lucky that they had not lived there then.

Many years later, Adik, Emma's middle brother, wrote: *"With my sister's ex-fiancé, Konstantin, I was always on good terms and met him even after 2000. He then worked in a boarding house "Rainbow" on Pervomaiskaya Street closer to the church. One day, he suggested that I correct my whirls on my head, and I agreed. And after that I often met him walking along the promenade."*

The longing for paternal love and care remained forever in Alena's heart, like an aching wound. Gradually, the subconscious desire to regain father's care turned into a passion for gaining man's loyalty. She took any smallest attention of men or their sexual attraction as love, and often received only suffering and a broken heart.

***

Flood

After heavy rains, in November 1954 severe flooding began. At that time, houses had simply trodden paths, and later, large stones were laid on them. There was a gutter near the walls of the windows of Emma's little house. During long torrential rains, water overflowed this ditch, churned along the paths, and rushed rapidly to the sea in a seething stream. On this day, water completely flooded the earthen floor of Emma's hut. A lot of her simple, poor belongings, and the first photos with her "groom" Konstantin disappeared in that black water. This severe flood also flooded the main street of Lenin near the sea. But the rain kept going and going, and the water rose to the very steps of the hairdresser, where Konstantin worked. Then he remembered his beloved with a child, huddled two blocks from the raging sea.

Seeing that the water is rising, the desperate Emma dressed her daughter in a plush coat and a white knitted hat with bells. She decided to move to her mother, who lived farther to the mountains, on the higher ground. Entering the hut of Emma, Konstantin looked encouragingly at his daughter and his beautiful, kind eyes smiled at her. Alena joyfully extended her hand to him, saying her first word: "Dad!" Father brought with him a rag doll Marfushka. It was single memory about him, and later Alena kept it for a long time.

At that moment, mad Emma screamed loudly in despair that her legs were already *"in the muddy streams of mountain's rivers."* And then, angrily pointing at Alena, she shouted with anguish: *"Here is your daughter, take her and get out of my life."* She furiously threw the little girl onto a hard sofa against the wall. Alena's coat slightly softened the impact. But still she felt a sharp pain in the lower part of the spine, and cried from all this unexpected horror. Later, doctors often asked Alena if she had ever had a spinal injury. But the memory for a long time erased from the consciousness of the child all the tragedies and pains of the past. After this terrible scene, ignoring more cries and reproaches from Emma, the miserable Konstantin left, and Alena never saw him again in their house.

***

Abandoned

Hopelessly gritting her teeth, Emma grabbed Alena in her arms, rushed through the horrible storm to her parents. She had nowhere to go. A sharp rain and an evil wind whipped the child in the face. Alena was unhappy and cold. But mother repeated through tears: *"Be patient, my little daughter."* And Alena believed that her mother still loved her, despite the recent cruel scene. Finally, after running a few blocks, Emma burst into the corridor of her parents. Her mother Anna ran out to meet her. Emma was in a frenzy, and sharply threw her daughter in the direction of her mother. She cried out in a torn voice: *"I can't live like that anymore!"*

For a moment, Alena felt herself somewhere freely falling down. But her grandmother still managed to pick up the girl almost near the floor. Suddenly, Emma's father jumped out of the room, red with anger. He yelled furiously at his unfortunate daughter, insulting and humiliating her: *"You dishonored me by messing up with the son of an enemy of the people! Get out of my house!"* But his wife Anna answered him, while trying as mush, as she could to protect her poor daughter Emma: *"Why? The son is not responsible for the father's unproven fault!"*

But Emma's father did not want to listen to them, cursing in disgusting words at the crying Emma. Unable to withstand all the troubles that fell on her, not finding shelter in the parents' house, Emma soon left. When she appeared again she sadly told her mother that she had already bought a ticket to Sakhalin, and would leave in the morning. And so Alena's lonely life began in the house of her good grandmother and her strict grandfather, whom she always feared "like a fire."

Later, father Konstantin tried to establish contact with Alena. But proud Emma always drove him away, depriving her daughter of her father's attention. Later, for some secret family circumstances, Alena received the name of her grandfather and was Filimonov for a while, and was recorded in her grandmother's passport as her own daughter. Alena's surname and patronymic changed several times, fundamentally turning her life around. New names brought new fates.

***

The close proximity of her lover (Alena's father), who betrayed her, was incredibly painful for Emma. Passionate by nature, for a long time Konstantin could not pacify his temper. He had several children with different women, but he continued to sleep around. His official wives, who always lived nearby, scandalized Emma for any reason, jealous of their past love. At times there were disputes about where the border between their tiny gardens was. Often, during the summer nights behind the fence, one could hear Konstantin's fights and battles with his next unhappy wife. Already in his late years in 1970th, one enterprising and judicious woman Valentina was able to finally curb the temperamental Konstantin. She also worked in the same organization as Alena's mother Emma. Later, Alena often saw his two new daughters. They, like all children of Konstantin, were very similar to their father and to each other. His youngest daughter Irina was about the same age as Lila, daughter of Alena. And later they often played together, living in the neighborhood. That's how all the necessary and unnecessary blood ties were intertwined into a tight ball. In Gelendzik almost all old families were relatives among themselves.

***

Once Upon a Time

Once, in 1996, Alena studied English at a private university in West Virginia. Every day, on her way to class, she passed through an art gallery. Some wise man hung reproductions of wonderful works of art on the wall so that everyone would admire them. Sometimes Alena stopped in front of her beloved "Portrait of a Young Girl" (Renoir) and thought about the amazing skill of the artist. The girl in the picture also watched Alena, following her wherever she went. Her beautiful deep eyes spoke of a happy, innocent purity, and looked at the world without fear.

Facing this portrait, Alena recalled herself as a child, and thought how naive she entered this world. An excess of trust and generosity also overwhelmed Alena's youth, and her eyes were wide open for good. Then she did not know fear, fear of loss and betrayal. When Alena occasionally looked at her childhood photographs, she saw there a little innocent girl looking at everyone with her big tear-stained eyes, as if asking: "Will you love me?" And she was sad with her.

The first fear comes to a child through the reaction of his mother to surrounding events. The child sees the frightened face of the mother, feels that his mother is afraid of something, and her fear is transmitted to him. Inside Alena, various fears were created by those who lived nearby. Her first and greatest fear came to her at a very early age, when she was no more than two years old. She always remembered the painful picture. Here she weeps in her grandmother's arms, and is struggling to break free. She beats like a wounded bird in the arms of her grandmother and kicks her. Realizing that this should not be happening, she, from terrible powerlessness, pounds with her fists the most beloved person, her grandmother, who is the only one who was always kind and affectionate to her. Alena screams to let her go after her retreating mother, walking away with her suitcases.

But only last night, Alena's mother promised to take her everywhere she would go, promised to take care of her. But then she took out her large suitcase and began to pack her things there. At the same time, Alena's things still were lying down in their places. Alena began to worry, brought her things to her mother, near her suitcase. *"Mommy! Please, take me with you! I will help you collect fish on the shore! I will do everything there for you. I will not bother you. Please don't just leave me alone. I feel so bad without you"*.

Mama promised to take Alena with her, but why were there tears in her eyes. Then mama puts Alena to bed, and quietly, in a breaking voice, sings a lullaby.

***

Broken Trust

The next morning Alena woke up too late, and heard an unusual silence in the house. Remembering that last night her mother packed her bags, she immediately shouted with alarm "mother!" But the house answered only with an empty echo. Not hearing the gentle voice of her mother, Alena ran out into the yard. There, her beloved mother had already gone out through the gate into the street. And her mother's brother Rema carried her suitcases. Alena rushed to the gate, screaming in agitation: *"You promised to take me with you!"*

But then grandmother ran up to Alena, grabbed her in her arms and pressed her to her chest. And mother left, not looking back at the heart-rending cries of her daughter.

Alena looked through her burning tears as her mother left, not understanding anything. She only knew that she could not live without her mother. She wanted to run after her, cling to the dress, hug and never part with her. Alena called her for a long time, crying from deep despair. But mother went farther and farther, and was no longer visible. At that moment, Alena's heart was breaking, suffering with fear and unexpected betrayal. Her grandmother was trying to calm, to comfort the child, but her loving words did not help.

This tragic moment of a great shock remained with Alena forever, because emotional memory is the strongest one. Alena's beautiful world of trust and love was destroyed. Grandmother's house was empty, as well as Alena's heart. A cruel lesson of fear, pain and betrayal crashed into the soul of the child. The moment of this sudden separation was like a terrible shock that the girl could never overcome. All her problems of the future came out of many childhood traumas, when she felt abandoned and unloved. This scar was pierced by a deep doubt in the love of loved ones, and the possibility of trusting anyone.

Alena's grandmother, seeing her despair, once said that they had to catch an airplane in order to get to her mother. At that time, on the other side of the bay there was an airport. The airplanes often turned near the grandmother's house, planning for the landing. Sometimes, early in the morning, hoping to fly to her mother, Alena collected her cubes and other simple toys, put them in a small bucket and ran out of the gate. There she stood for a long time and looked up at the sky.

Sometimes the plane flew quite low. Alena was sure that the pilot could hear her, and she shouted to her with all her might, her head up to the sky: *"Pilot, pilot! Take me to mother in Sakhalin!"* But the airplane flew by without landing on the glade near her grandmother's house. Alena's grandfather Minai stood at the gate, looked at her and giggled. Apparently, she was doing something wrong, and she was bitter.

***

Escape

For several days Alena thought that her mother would return "soon", as she was promised. Therefore, she took her little bench, stood on it, looking out the window until dark. She did not go to eat or play her favorite games. She just stood there and waited for her mother, feeling that she was very vulnerable, and had absolutely no protection. But in the evening the grandmother approached, and took the girl by the hand: *"We should first buy a fur coat, baby; it's always cold in Sakhalin"*. Grandmother tried to come up with various reassuring stories in order to distract Alena from thinking about her mother, who promised to take her, but who had left alone.

One summer, a helicopter landed near the grandmother's house on a meadow, and everyone ran to it. Alena was curious if this helicopter could reach Sakhalin. She, quietly walked next to a woman, got inside, hid under a chair and sat there, until the helicopter took off. And then she got out, sat in the chair, enjoying the view from the window. Then, the Stuart found her: - *"Whose are you? Where do you live?"* -

And Alena showed them down: *"I live down in the garden; my house is the second from the corner! Look, over there my grandmother runs across the field and waves us joyfully. But I need to see my mother on Sakhalin!"*

The helicopter made a big circle over the city, and then it was landed back in the meadow. A crying grandmother ran up. She was happy that Alena was found, that at least she had not been stolen as last time. And Alena's grandfather was very angry again. So, when Alena and her grandmother returned home, they sat quietly, embracing, away from her grandfather, reading a book.

Days and weeks passed. So autumn came with its rains. All the time, Alena felt sad, miserable and lonely, as if she lived in a desert. Alena so wanted to see her mother's beautiful face. Every day she continued to stand by the window on the terrace, or in the room by the glass front door. She was afraid to miss mom's return. For her, "soon" meant an hour later; in extreme cases, maybe tomorrow. And once suddenly, it looked like, Alena saw her, so beautiful and so proud, walking around the courtyard in her astrakhan coat, warming her hands in the coupling. Alena was surprised that mom had this old-fashioned, winter clutch, although it was raining outside. Only for some reason mother did not go to the house, but turned to the well, which stood at the neighbor's fence.

- *Mother! I'm here*! - shouted Alena with all her might.

- *Alenochka, my dear, what is wrong with you?* - the grandmother's frightened voice came.

- *There is mom!* My *mother is in the yard! I saw her! Open the door faster! Otherwise she went to the neighbors!*

Alena beat her slender little bodies in the glass door, calling her mother. But then her stool suddenly turned upside down, and Alena fell down, hit hard on the side of it, and lost consciousness. She remained in this state for a long time. When she regained consciousness she again returned to the glass door, desperately waiting for the promised "soon" return of her mother. She did not want to eat, drink or play for a long time.

Only rubber boots reminded of mom. They were old-fashioned boots with a special recess for the heel. Mom wore them on her beautiful shoes when, in rainy weather, she went to work. Now they lonely clung to the corner on the terrace. Beside them was still standing a navy blue, old convertible stroller. Alena remembered how her mother once pushed her in this stroller somewhere. At that moment, Alena tried to look outside the edge of the raised hood of the stroller to see what was happening around. Any trip to the city from the cramped, dark grandmother's house was a happy adventure for Alena. But her mother raised that hood of the stroller, and it prevented Alena from enjoying the outside world. Alena was upset. At that time, she still could not talk well and just was crying. Her mother was angry with no reason, shouted at her, saying that it was time to sleep. Alena, swallowing tears from an undeserved angry shout, obediently lay at the bottom of the stroller, not wanting to upset her mother. Not finding warmth and tenderness around in the place where she lived, Alena ceased to smile unreasonably and happily.

***

Secrets

Winter passed. The pain of loss plunged deeply into the subconscious. Alena tried not to think anymore, and not to ask about her mother. Then spring came with its awakening fragrant nature. And then came her favorite, fun summer, when Alena was finally allowed to go out to play outside. There she spent most of her time hiding from the world among tall flowers or in thickets of fragrant bushes. There she learned a special way to protect herself against offenders. This was taught by a bee. Despite her subsequent death, she deftly took revenge by stinging the attacker.

Most of the year Alena was spending outside, with no control, watch or care by the adults. There she learned how to understand the language of animals and birds, and spoke with them on equal terms. Sitting on warm earth, drowning in the wonderful smell of wildflowers, she spent long hours watching the hard work of the harmonious society of the zealous and defenseless ants. Then she thought that maybe someone out there high above the world of people also follows their actions and can punish the negligent at any moment.

Living without her mother, Alena was for a long time often sick, often fell out of bed, and saw dreams where she was flying. Also, she was a "night walker" - she walked during her sleep without waking up. Her grandmother knew it and watched her, trying to be sure that Alena would not commit something dangerous to her life in her sleep walk. It often happened, when the moon was big, that Alena's grandmother often found her somewhere far in the garden, and gently would talk to her, and bring her back to the house. The first conscious grief of her earlier childhood settled in Alena's soul a deep distrust of people, and of everyone around. All her feelings were aggravated, and she became incredibly suspicious. While watching all people around, she constantly tried to understand what they think and how they relate to her. It was during this period that she began to deeply doubt that someone really loved her. Alena's attitude to others and her own behavior depended on what Alena thought and felt about people.

From early childhood, two terrible beasts settled in her heart: loneliness and separation. It seemed that only they alone belonged to her completely, and were the only ones who did not betray. Life around her was full of contradictions and secrets, and little Alena fought alone with her inner demons. Every day was filled with various fears. She often took conscious and unconscious risk with one desire: to excel. She needed to stand out, to overcome something, to be ahead of everyone, to be better than everyone, so that only she would finally be noticed and respected. Often, fighting for the opportunity to feel the care of loved ones, and fearing them, Alena tried to defend herself by simply smiling at everything that was happening or hiding silently. She realized very early that even the closest people inflicted mental pain and she tried to avoid them. More and more rejecting the outside world, she closed herself in, not trusting anyone, but still expecting some kind of miracle.

After the tragedies of childhood and too early mental trauma, Alena experienced several complexes. One of them was the fear of being late somewhere. It came to her that one morning when her mother left home while Alena was still sleeping. This strong fear of "not being late" lived forever inside her. It was so old and so strong that even when Alena was delayed for only one or two minutes, she already felt unpleasant stress. Therefore, she tried to come everywhere in advance. Later analyzing the events of distant childhood, Alena unraveled their roots.

***

Relatives

Greek great-grandmother Maria lived only one block from Emma's house and two blocks from Grandmother Anna's house. She seemed a very old, dark and dried up woman. Only her big, black eyes were very alive and shined with a very strong light. One might have felt that her eyes could burn you alive, if she only wished it. Anyway, she moved slowly, helping herself with a crutch, and looked like a sorceress from the fairy tale Sleeping Beauty.

Despite her strange appearance, she was very kind to Alena, and the girl felt that the old-old great-grandmother Maria really loved her. When they passed by her house, she tried to pat Alena on the head with her thin, bony hand, and often secretly shoved candy or even money into Alena's pocket. Alena thought that she was purposefully sitting there, on her corner with one goal - to meet Alena. Great-grandmother Maria often whispered meaningfully in Alena's ears: *"Don't worry about anything. I passed you a very special gift. You have a very bright future, and always will get whatever you want. Your beauty is a powerful force. Use that gift carefully;*

do not waste it in vain. And I will always protect you, my beautiful child."

Then, they talked for a while with Alena's Russian grandmother. After that, all the way to Emma's house, grandmother Anna was silent and looked very serious, like she learned some mystical wisdom, closed to her before that. Unfortunately, with each year, Alena's mother and grandmother tried to prevent Alena from communicating with her Greek relatives. But in a small town it was impossible to hide something.

Gradually Alena became acquainted with her Greek relatives, and dreamed that they openly recognized her as their own. The Greeks often met her on the streets, talked about their ancient family, and about other members of the huge clan. In Alena's heart they created the feeling that she should be proud of her ancient Greek roots, which originated in the family of King Constantine. Especially kind was her father's sister, Olga, who lived nearby. It was her aunt Olga who brought up a spirit of pride in Alena for her own beauty and self-esteem. She helped her to believe in her own strengths and overcome the problems of "abandonment" and alienation Alena always felt while growing up.

Only in the summer it was relatively good to be living in the poor and small house of her Russian grandmother. Her grandmother Anna was very hospitable. So, every summer many relatives came to her to relax by the sea without paying her anything. Alena rejoiced at people who had nothing to hide from her. To Alena's questions about her father, they answered her that he was a long-distance sailor. She believed this and was waiting for him. For street walks, Alena was often dressed up in a beautiful marine suit. She was very proud of it, thinking that this outfit was sent to her by a loving father, and this brought them together. In the port area, there were a lot of sailors walking in the evenings, wearing flared trousers. Alena's height was to their knees, and while walking with her mother along the street, she grabbed the bottom of their wide trousers. And then, with her head up, she asked: *"Have you met my father?"* But the sailors only smiled back and passed by. Once one of them crouched and affectionately asked her name, gaily glancing at the beautiful mother. For Alena, this attention was like a victory. She was convinced that the sailor stopped nearby only for her own sake. Then she thought: *"Or maybe he is my dad?"*

Grandmother Anna told her daughter Emma that the pride and s love to a man fight inside the souls of a woman. She was very angry with the reckless choice of her daughter Emma, and with her choice to be with Alena's father Konstantin. Also, she was angry with her own husband Mina, who had several illegitimate children in Gelendzhik. Generally, grandmother often spoke negatively about all men of the world, probably for Alena's educational purposes. Or maybe she just wanted to share her sorrows with at least someone, and only the little granddaughter was her silent listener. Grandmother Anna, raising Alena, did not particularly think that her negative grunts would shape the girl's life. Alena absorbed her grandmother's character and views. She grew up with a hostile attitude towards men, believing, following her grandmother, that all men are second-class people who can do nothing but children, and therefore do not deserve much respect.

For several years, mother Emma lived and worked in Sakhalin. She rented a room at her uncle Ivan Pugachev (Filimonov). He also once had a fight with his brother Minai on the political issues, and left Gelendzhik forever. Only a few years later, when Alena had almost forgotten her mother, she suddenly returned. But communication and trust were undermined, and she seemed to Alena completely alien. In addition, her mother brought with her a young stepfather Gregory, who immediately disliked an independent and proud girl.

In the early 1960s, having received permission from the city authorities, mother and stepfather began to build a large house on the spot where Emma's old shack was once. They were completely absorbed in building that house, and in their lives, rarely paying attention to a seven-year-old girl. Alena, as before, was left to herself. Over time, Emma's new home, conveniently located in a wonderful place, two blocks from the sea, began to arouse envy. Many people desired to take possession of it. So there were new problems that captured Emma, and in the fight against them, the daughter was again in last place.

***

Pearls

The whirlwinds of fate, like the waves of a raging ocean, took off and fell, dragging a person along, and continuing to weave their invisible, connecting threads.

One day in the early 2000s, Alena and her American husband Victor were on a comfortable cruise ship. In general, they traveled a lot together, especially in the first ten years of their surprisingly harmonious and happy life. Once, their huge, sixteen-story ocean liner had been hanging out in the South Pacific for more than a week. In this foggy water expanse without borders, strange sensations and thoughts visited Alena. But there was a lot of entertainment on the ship, so there was no time to yearn or be bored. Every day they went to concerts and various lectures. Alena was especially interested in hearing about pearls. It was said that the main characteristic of pearls is that they don't overshadow their owner, but only emphasizes her natural attractiveness and femininity. It is no accident that pearls have always been a symbol of purity, innocence and restraint. The frames of icons, church vestments, altars and bindings of the Bibles were decorated with pearls. Also, for some mysterious reason, pearls have always had a strong influence on Alena.

Finally, the huge liner reached one of the small islands of the Pacific Ocean called Bora Bora. Walking along the shore, they saw sellers of pearls, and bought some beautiful strands of white and black pearls.

Returning to the ship, Alena did not part with the beads. She fingered them, like a rosary, stroked and felt that something incredibly familiar was blowing from them. For that foggy night in the Pacific Ocean, Alena for some reason could not sleep.

The ocean has always had a strange, even mysterious influence on Alena. And suddenly, in the quiet night of the vast ocean, the tightly-closed draperies of her childhood memory rose, and she remembered why she was so attracted to pearls. She finally found the courage to look behind the black wings of a deep veil. A shocking discovery occurred in the Pacific Ocean. Alena clearly saw her mother, again standing in front of her in her favorite pearls. She suddenly remembered the secret of her mother's priceless pearl beads. Then only did Alena realize what kind precious jewelry she had lost. She could not sleep that night on the American ship. She saw that some of these beautiful beads still seemed to lie next to her, the little girl Alena. They crashed into her memory with a sorrowful symbol of a lost treasure, a symbol of broken love and unfulfilled happiness. A painful childhood memory wounded her soul with the acuteness of heavy losses, and shed tears on her pillow in their comfortable luxury cabin.

***

Lost Treasure

For many years, in a closet of the Leningrad apartment, Alena kept amazing, completely round, heavy, white pearls. Each pearl was about sixteen millimeters in diameter. Between the pearls were solid wax nodules that separate and protect them from colliding with each other. However, this long string of pearls was torn in several places and wrapped in an old handkerchief. They were special pearls, grown for many decades and mysteriously glowing from the inside. It was impossible to take your eyes off of them. Alena's grandmother called them "Pearls of Mikimoto." The incredibly beautiful necklace of rare pearls was a real masterpiece that Alena did not even suspect. It was a sad memory for her about her mother who had left so early.

Once, in the Pacific Ocean, a shocking discovery occurred. Alena suddenly remembered the secret of priceless pearl beads. Then only did Alena realize what kind of jewelry she had lost. . She saw that some of these beautiful beads still seemed to lay next to her, the little girl Alena. They crashed into her memory with a sorrowful symbol of a lost treasure, a symbol of broken love and unfulfilled happiness. A painful childhood memory wounded her soul with the acuteness of heavy losses, and shed tears on her pillow in their comfortable luxury cabin.

***

In one of her old albums, Alena stored a very old photograph from 1959. In this photo, she recalled her incredibly beautiful mother, who so much hoped for happiness, smiled slightly, as sad as a smile of Giaconda. The photograph was supposed to symbolize the beginning of a new family, which, after many years of separation, Emma planned to create by bringing a "new dad" for Alena from Sakhalin Island. But the deeply wounded daughter, who for a long time had been waiting for her mother, was jealous of her stranger. And when she came back, she still disappeared to somewhere or spent time with her new husband. All of Alena's hopes for her mother's care and attention were in vain.

On that day going to take a memorable photo, everyone dressed up. Photography in general was a big event for people at that time. For this occasion, mother specially wore precious beads made of stunning white pearls. These beads were so long that she wrapped them around her neck twice, and then, she tied them into a small spectacular knot.

Either because mother was in a hurry, or because she did not know how to do it before, Emma quickly poked her daughter's beautiful hair with a sharp comb, and stuck a white bow on her head. Then Alena began to be forced to wear a new, "crepe de Chine" dress, which her stepfather chose for her. But this dress was shamefully transparent, unpleasantly prickly and simply shapeless. Alena had an innate craving for beauty, and her grandmother instilled in her a taste for simple, comfortable things. The girl immediately disliked this indefinite color outfit and did not want to wear it. But her mother forced her to do this contrary to the wishes of the child, not reckoning with the feelings of her daughter, but only to please her new husband. Alena hopelessly obeyed, crying with despair. And then, all the way to the city Alena was very upset. In the photo shop she wouldn't want to stand next to this stranger and smile to him.

From the day one, the stepfather immediately began to smugly and rudely bring her up. And then, on this solemn day, which was supposed to be a celebration for everyone, he began to "lecture" and teach Alena's mother, loudly expressing his dissatisfaction with the girl's behavior. The good mood was spoiled. Alena saw that her beloved mother was very upset by his negative nit-picking and disagreement with her daughter. But most of all, Alena was outraged by the behavior of this man, stinking of beer. Although, he was younger than her mother, he dared to dictate what she should do with her own child.

A rude, narrow-minded person who had just burst into their lives caused her rejection. Alena considered him an empty place, and was sure that he had no right to scold her. A five-year-old girl was defenseless, but she deeply understood everything around her. At that moment, when he spoiled her joy for taking photo with her mother, she was swallowing the bitter tears of disrespect for her personality. She answered him rudely, but while glancing at her mother for help. She was looking for mother's protection. Alena could not believe that her mother would choose a stranger instead of her child. It was the same terrible betrayal that Alena had already experienced from her once before. A few years ago, mother broke her promise, and left her, going to this Gregory. From that moment, Alena hated that Gregory forever.

A 1959 photograph forever captured the stepfather's angry, evil face and sad mother, still hopefully trying to smile. Alena stood there, offended, with tears in her eyes. She did not want to hug anyone, uncomfortably and tightly sandwiched between two adults who dreamed of their own happiness. There was no place for an illegitimate child who was always a reproach and a reminder of the mistakes of youth.

***

Broken Promises

Soon, mother disappeared again. Once again, as always, Alena played alone in her grandmother's house. She often came into this "cold" room and stayed there for hours. She enjoyed opening the drawers, and examining her mother's things that were stored there. When the longing for her mother especially greatly angered her soul, Alena even looked inside a small old closet. Almost all the things in the closet smelled like mothballs. But her mother's few dresses smelled of her favorite perfume "Red Moscow". For the girl it was like the smell of her mother. She loved to caress and feel these dresses with the smell of her mother. At such moments, it seemed to her that her mother was nearby, did not leave anywhere at all, and did not miss so many events of her childhood.

Once Alena could not resist and, despite all her grandmother's terrifying prohibitions, she took out from the closet her mother's favorite necklace. For Alena, these pearls were magical. She heard that these beads were sacredly kept under lock and key because they were a gift from her Greek father. This fact reinforced for Alena the significance and value of the necklace. Alena quietly played with pearls, sitting on the couch, stroking and kissing beads. Although she felt that she was doing something forbidden, she still could not stop. She admired this precious memory of her mother. Suddenly, grandmother entered the room. Alena realized that she was caught red-handed, and, frightened, immediately hid the necklace behind her, quickly pushing it under the pillow. And grandmother, in a fright, screamed angrily at her, grabbed the beads and began to pull them to herself. Alena was indignant at the harshness of her usually loving and affectionate grandmother. She held the beads tightly, and also shouted:

"No, I won't give it to you! *These are my mother's beads. I have the right to just touch them."*

They pulled the string of beads in different directions, and no one wanted to concede. And suddenly the priceless necklace exploded. Snow-white, perfectly round, one to one, with a loud bang, pearls were falling on the bare wooden floor. Heavy balls of pearls pounded hopelessly and tragically, like Alena's heart, and rolled under the sofa. Grandmother and Alena sobbed at the same time, each on her own occasion. One cried bitterly from torn beauty and the other from her ruined life. And suddenly, out of nowhere, Alena's mother ran into the room into the noise. Seeing what happened, her face changed and darkened. But she did not say anything, did not swear. But she did not try to comfort the child, either. Grandmother whispered timidly through tears: *"Maybe we could take them to a jewelry workshop and fix it?"*

"No, you can't," said mother. *They would be stolen."*

Some of these beautiful beads still lay next to Alena. They crashed into her memory a woeful symbol of a lost treasure, a symbol of broken love and unfulfilled happiness.

***

Looses

Once in 1994, before leaving Russia, Alena decided to fix her mother's pearl string. She took them to a jewelry store in Leningrad. The receptionist behind the window, glancing quickly at the beads, immediately went into the other room, hidden by the curtains. Soon an old, fat and unpleasant store owner came out. When he saw the old pearl beads, his hands began to tremble. But Alena did not pay special attention to this. He spoke irritably to her, demandingly asking where she had taken these beads. Alena suddenly, as in childhood, was frightened by his unreasonably rude voice, so similar to the evil voice of her stern grandfather, punishing her for all the wrongdoings. Alena quietly replied to the Jew jeweler: *"My mother *died. And now it remains ..."*

After a pause, and not releasing the precious pearls from his thick, sweaty fingers, the jeweler barked that he would collect the pearls with a new thread, replacing the broken one. *"Come back in a week,"* he snapped rudely, and somehow strangely began to put Alena on the street. Alena left this store with a heavy feeling. She could not find peace and could not sleep, thinking that she had done something irreparable. She returned to this jewelry store a few days later and was immediately given the same length of white "pearl". She was very surprised at his lightness, and said that this was not what she left with them. But the woman in the window began to resent and hiss at Alena, claiming that everything was right. *"Take what you got and get out,"* she muttered roughly, but firmly.

Rudeness and insults always shocked Alena. If someone insulted her or showed her cruelty, she was always very lost and stiff. So it was this time. Alena realized with horror that the jeweler, as her mother had warned many years ago, replaced precious pearls with white plastic balls. At that terrible moment of this stunning discovery, Alena with terrible fear realized that she had been robbed. The rare pearls of her mother were taken away. But most importantly, they robbed her from the only precious memory of her mother.

Alena's grandmother carefully preserved these priceless pearls for many decades after the early death of her daughter Emma. A beautiful necklace kept many memories. It was a symbol of Alena's mother's first love. It was a memory of Alena's waiting, and the symbol of her hope. For a long time, Alena with her own daughter Lila was starving, suffering and living in poverty. At the same time, a treasure wrapped in a simple, old handkerchief was kept in her Leningrad apartment. No one ever suspected its real value. Then, the pearl beads so irrevocably were gone forever.

***

Probably due to the deep wounds of her childhood, Alena was always deeply focused on her feelings and emotions, constantly delving into her experiences. Living deep inside herself, she seemed to live life in "pink glasses", looking at everything, as if from the outside, as a spectator.

Many years have passed since this last tragic case of Russian life. And then one day in the Pacific Ocean, Alena's kind husband bought her a gift, a beautiful string of white pearls. When Alena saw its true price, she was enormously surprised and gasped. Her memory, which had kept the pain of childhood grievances for so long, suddenly returned to her, burning with the bitterness of her lost pearls. Alena infinitely regretted that throughout her life in Russia she was so blind and knew so little real life. It was a severe shock that struck her in the Pacific Ocean.

The ocean was still the same. He also washed the shores of the distant island of Sakhalin, where once her mother escaped from adversity. Emma lived and worked for a long time off the Pacific coast. And in Gelendzhik she was awaited by delightful pearls, a generous symbol of her first love. This ocean knew the hands and love of her mother. And this ocean once returned to Alena the indelible pain of irreparable, deepest loss. But the past is always too late and useless to regret. Everything disappeared, everyone left, disappeared forever. Life repeated the only wisdom: if there is love, it must be protected. We must love and protect those who are near. But people do not learn this lesson. Alena also could not teach this to those whom she loved more than anything.

Binding Threads

In mid-August 1961, Alena stood at a low window, looking into the garden and listening to the radio. She did not want to leave her childhood house where she was raised by her loving grandmother Anna. But this August, there were big changes in her life. It was the last carefree summer. Recently, her mother with a new husband returned to Gelendzhik. In place of Emma's old shack, they built a large, beautiful house. Soon Alena was supposed to move into it to live. But this was not good news for Alena. She hated the unpleasant, thin-lipped stepfather. From the first day he "exercised" his rights, sharply indicating to his mother how she should deal with her daughter. They immediately had conflicts, and in his disputes with Alena, his mother treacherously took his side, trying to please her new husband in everything. Alena could not forgive mother for that betrayal.

Sometimes, for a show, expressing his "care", her step father took the child Alena to his lap and whispered some compliments. But this was extremely unpleasant, because soon under Alena something swelled getting bigger. It was a shame to sit on his lap, and Alena fled in a panic. Her relatives were surprised at her bad manners, called her "wild", and no one listened to the little girl's arguments. Despite her stubborn resistance, in the new conditions Alena had to follow what was decided without her participation.

In this autumn another significant event was coming. In September, Alena was going to go to her first grade of school. But this event did not look good either for the freedom-loving girl. She heard from her friends on the street that the teachers were strict, controlling everything in the school, asking all sorts of lessons. In addition, they will force her to do everything that Alena did not like to do at all. These disturbing thoughts flashed through the head of a girl standing by the window.

Suddenly the announcer indignantly announced the shocking news. Twenty-year-old American student Victusha and his friend tried to hide a girl in the trunk of their car in order to transport her from East Berlin to West. But they were stopped, searched and sent to prison. The boy's grandmother named Emma, as all his relatives, was terribly worried and tried to help him.

Coincidentally, she had the same name as Alena's mother. It shocked Alena. At the same time, while listening to Soviet radio, hysterically condemning American students, Alena could not imagine that in some magical way, thirty-five years later, this boy Victusha would become her devoted and loving husband. Invisible, binding threads rushed to the other end of the earth, across the ocean, continued to weave the paths of fate and connect the future with the present.

Some years later, in summer, Alena walked with the girls who rented a room in her mother's house. They chatted merrily, not paying any attention to the teenager, and had fun with the famous game of "cities". The most difficult thing was that each new city had to start with the same letter that the name of the previous city ended with. But soon their knowledge of the cities ran out, and the game stopped. Then they began to express their cherished dreams aloud, boasting about those amazing places where each of them would like to live. One girl arrogantly said that she would live "only in the capital of our country." And everyone looked at her with envy, because she dreamed of something incredible, like from a fairy tale.

At that time, many residents of the province dreamed of living in the more prosperous and exciting Moscow. But it was almost impossible. However, her mother's younger brother Reanold already lived in Moscow, and also two grandmothers' brothers lived there. After the Second World War (1941-1945), her grandmother for a long time searched for her relatives, and she found them ten years later. In winter, leaving from the cruelty of her husband, who slept around, she took Alena to visit them. So, Alena knew what Moscow was. She had no desire to live there, in a cold, noisy, fussy and huge city. But talking about it aloud to the fussy girls would be foolish. Nevertheless, Alena wanted to quickly announce something unusual, so that they would pay attention to her and show some respect. Then, Alena loudly and firmly declared: *"And I will live in America!"*

In the 1960s, during the outbreak of the Cold War with America, to wish such strange thing and in a loud voice was simply outrageous revolutionary blasphemy. So, everyone just maliciously laughed at such an awkward, wild joke, continuing on their way, and not looking anymore at the daring girl. If they had only known that the Lord heard these words, and fulfilled everything. Many years later it happened.

In the meantime, to sensitive and sharp-eyed Alena, her own life continued to bring many downs and ups, joys and tragedies. Invisible, connecting threads continued to weave the paths of fate and to connect the future with the present. The whirlwinds of fate, like the waves of a raging ocean, took off and fell, dragging a person along, and continuing to weave their invisible, connecting threads.

The whirlwinds of fate, like the waves of a raging ocean, took off and fell, dragging a person along, and continuing to weave their invisible, connecting threads. And then, when Alena was also only twenty years old, she experienced a situation similar to Victusha, when he was only twenty. For a short time, but she ended up in a Soviet prison, so similar to the Berlin prison.

***

Berlin Prison

After the defeat of fascist Germany, the territory of Berlin was divided into two zones. The eastern part was under the influence of the USSR. The western part of Berlin was under the United States, Britain and France. At first, the border between the western and eastern parts of Berlin was open, and thousands of people crossed it daily. They could compare living conditions of two parts of Berlin. In August 1960, West Germany refused a trade agreement with the eastern part of the country. East Germany was regarded it as an "economic war." On August 13, 1961, the Berlin Wall was built there, which lasted until 1989. This happened just two weeks before the trip by Victusha and his fellow countryman Gilb to Berlin. Prior to this, Victusha attended a summer school in Oslo, and his friend studied in France. Gilb learned that Victusha had a fashionable Volkswagen car, and suggested meeting him in Berlin during the summer vacation and going on a trip around Germany. Although the world was in a difficult political situation, American tourists could easily cross the border between East and West Berlin. Their passports were checked, but the car was usually not searched. At that time, Volkswagen was one of the most popular cars in Germany, and it was called a "People's Car". The car was painted it mainly in all shades of blue or red. Defiantly red Volkswagen was very popular in America. One of the agricultural organizations, with which father of Victusha collaborated, offered to buy this quality machine for them. They asked Victusha to buy the red Volkswagen and send it to America across the ocean.

In East Berlin the public telephones were cheap, and one day, the guys decided to call home in California. At the post office, the employee demanded a special document confirming on what grounds the students own the currency, and where they received it from. From an unexpected obstacle and the injustice of the demand, the quick-tempered Gilbert entered into a rather sharp argument with the clerk. But the clerk did not understand English well, and the guys did not know German. But then suddenly a German student Erica hastened to their aid. She stood in the line behind them, and volunteered to be their translator. But the clerk was already furious with the behavior of "arrogant American snobs." The guys did not have a document for currency, and they could not call home. Gilb and Victusha left the post office and the girl immediately left after them. After they left, the mail clerk most likely immediately called the security service, telling about the incident.

Leaving the post office, the guys were very upset and vigorously discussed the incident. With keen sympathy for them, Erica offered to act as their guide, and show new friends areas of East Berlin that had not yet been completely restored after the war. Having talked, she complained about the construction of a wall that separated her family and her lover. Knowing that she was very at risk, the fragile girl still tried to put pressure on the guys' pity, taking advantage of their inexperience. She even managed to confuse their head with a story that she plans to escape to the Western part of Berlin in a tourist bus. It seemed even to the romantic American students quite implausible. They began to politely admonish her so that she would not do such stupidity. Then she, as if casually, hinted that this could be done in the trunk of their car.

Cautious Victusha at first flatly refused. Given the international tension and the outbreak of the Cold War, young Victusha strongly doubted the reasonableness of what the energetic adventurer Gilb suggested he do. Grieving, Erica nevertheless asked to send at least a letter to her relatives in the forbidden part of the city. Although this was also illegal, but Victusha, reluctantly agreed, yielding to the onslaught of his two opponents.

The next day, the guys, having delivered the letter and safely returned to the communist Eastern part of the city, met with Erica. Then she again, word for word, began to convince them to transport her to the other side. Doubts about the rationality of such a rash act greatly tormented Victusha's soul. And he quietly said that the trunk is very small, and she will not fit there. But the stubborn Gilb puffed up and ranted, wanting to show himself a hero, convincing Victusha that it was safe and easy to do. In the end, Victusha, by his natural gentleness, yielded to persuasion. Erica, for security reasons, suggested meeting at night on a quiet street to hide in the trunk without prying eyes. Although the trunk was tiny, the fragile girl somehow, with joy, fit in there.

In East Berlin crammed with spies. It looked, like even the houses had eyes and ears. They began their journey across the border at about ten in the night. This clearly seemed suspicious to the border guard, and was another irreparable mistake. When students arrived at a checkpoint in a red

Volkswagen, they were immediately stopped. The border guards asked them to open the trunk and found Erica there. The irreparable happened. East German soldiers arrested them, sent to a prison, and the car was confiscated. Young Americans were brought into the common room, where they met with two Sudanese students, British and Dutch merchants, who were caught for about the same "crime". Officials interrogated everyone and sentenced to two years in prison. Victusha regretted about his participation in that event all his life. Newspapers of many countries were full of headlines: "German Reds imprison two American students" and "Red sentence to 2 American youths for escape". And communist propaganda shouted condemningly about "the shame of American spies."

  Only after some time, Victusha's father suddenly found out about the arrest of his son. A dumbfounded neighbor called him in horror, and said that something completely unbelievable had happened with his son Victusha. At that time, most Americans were busy with their peaceful lives distant from European problems. So Victusha's family had the most "superficial" idea of the strange wall dividing Berlin. They were simply terribly frightened by the unprecedented cruelty of the verdict for their so obedient son, accustomed to living by the rules. Desiring to immediately release him, his father began to look for all sorts of ways to do this. He talked with different people who had at least some influence in East Germany. Then, he flew to Berlin several times. At the same time, Victusha's father understood the senselessness of seeking help from the US government. At that time, the United States had not yet recognized the Eastern Germany government. "If we had a US representative there, they would very quickly release my son," - his father later said.

  Help came from the influential Sunkist Growers organization, with which Victusha's father had long, close contacts, selling his oranges through them. The Sunkist distribution center was both in West Germany and in France. One of the officials of this organization exchanged West German goods for East German goods, and knew someone in the government of East

Germany. Also, this man Brans found a German lawyer for the arrested guys because the East German government did not recognize the American family lawyer for Victusha's defense.

A lawyer from East Berlin spent a week with his Victusha's father, helping him to write a letter to the head of Communist government of East Germany. This letter was to be written only in German, emphasizing respect for the nation (as the lawyer emphasize). Although for Victusha's father, a true American from head to toe, it was incredibly difficult to do, the letter was written in such a way as to cajole and flatter Walter Ulbricht. The letter said that two romantic boys, not understanding the seriousness of the crime, simply out of nobleness, made a mistake. And that American people hope that *"the great father of the German Republic will forgive the guys for what they did and set them free."*

But Ulbricht decided to use American students as an example to show the world that the new socialist government of East Germany cannot be played the fool. Only after four months, with great difficulty, it became possible to release Victusha and Gilb from the German prison. They stayed there longer than Sudanese students and traders from other countries.

The first, most terrible month, Victusha spent there, in a solitary, concrete cell. Its width was equal to his open arms, and it was about 10 feet long. The toilet was a bucket (barrel) in the corner. Victusha slept on a rotten, worn, thatched mattress, which was thrown onto a slightly raised, concrete platform. Sometimes he managed to get some nonsense book, a German textbook and a bible. Only once a week the guards let him out into the narrow courtyard for a walk, and sometimes giving him a shovel for work. Shovel for Victusha was a familiar tool, and he perceived this obligation rather as entertainment, and happily worked. In the silence of the solitary confinement, Victusha continued to convince himself that it would all be over soon. It never crossed his mind that in reality, everything was much more serious than he had supposed. In 1986, he recalled: *"I lost a lot of weight. My teeth hurt from hard bread and sausages. Once we were given several slices of tomato and onion. It seemed to me an incredible delicacy, and I asked for more. But they refused me."*

Relatives were allowed to visit their twenty-year-old, exhausted son only after a month of his imprisonment. "He looked like a corpse, it was just awful to look at him," his father recalled. After a month of being in a solitary hole, his father managed to have Victusha transferred to a common cell with six people. The spacious chamber had more acceptable conditions for existence. But its main advantage was the luxury of human communication.

Once, while walking through the prison, Victusha caught a glimpse of Erica. But she walked far down the corridor and did not notice him. Four months later, when Victusha and Gilb were ordered to change clothes for release, in the prison closet they saw the same coat of Erica which she wore on the day of her arrest. She was still in prison. Her punishment was harsher; there was no one to intercede for her.

These tragic events in a German prison shocked Victusha a lot. Shame and guilt haunted him for a long time. Most likely, therefore, a sensitive and sentimental man, Victusha married early, passionately seeking solace, love and understanding. But it was his naive mistake of youth, as he recalled many years later. Returning from Germany, Victusha forever blocked the memory of those terrible events of his youth, not wanting to remember or talk about his suffering. These sad events of his youth did not allow him to feel like a big hero, as the American press wanted to describe. Once, he finally gave an interview about his painful time in prison. Explaining his behavior in Germany, already a forty-five-year-old, highly respected person, the director of several organizations, Victusha said: *"I have been asked many times if I would do it again. That would depend on my knowledge of the consequences. I don't know how to put it, not sounding like a "super patriot". But there was someone who suffered in the framework of the system that we considered unfair. We had the opportunity for direct intervention. And we did it."*

Victusha's friends, speaking of his character, emphasized that without hesitation he always upheld what he considered to be right. One of his friend, a citrus producer, Rick once emphasized that "Victusha is a first-class guy." Continuing the work of his great-grandfather, grandfather and father, Victusha was engaged in agriculture since childhood, growing oranges and avocados. He traveled a lot around the world, sharing his experience and knowledge. East German officials invited him to their country, but Victusha did not have the slightest desire to visit them.

***

Such events took place with American guy Victusha in 1961. At the same time, seven-year-old Alena stood at the window of her grandmother's house, listening to the radio. Already long ago, invisible threads of fate stretched across the Pacific Ocean and connected them with each other. But they still did not know this at all. Each of them will live own life, with all its ups and downs. They will walk towards each other a long way, and finally, one day, they will happily unite.

***

Alena's Arrest

During long time anybody could get into the Russian prison with no proven fault. This is why there was a proverb "don't announce that you would not be in the prison or would not be a beggar". This could happen to anybody at any time. The whirlwinds of fate, like the waves of a raging ocean, took off and fell, carrying the man along with him. They continued to weave their invisible, connecting threads between Alena and Victusha, between the present and the future. When Alena was also only twenty years old, she also experienced a situation similar to Victor.

***

Alena grew up a mischievous, extremely inquisitive and very impressionable child. Due to the circumstances of her birth and the situation of her family, the girl from an early age lived in an atmosphere of secrecy and confusion. But she had a deep instinct, intuition, and did not tolerate any secrets around her. When she felt that something was hiding from her, then by all means, she tried to solve it and did not stop until all secret became clear. This often led her into much trouble. But she could not do anything about it, keenly and skeptically perceiving the world, and did not trust anyone. Later, the cold attitude of her family was aggravated by her hated stepfather, making her life in mother's house simply unbearable. Having no close relationship with her mother, Alena spent time reading books, twisted in the illusions of a fictional world, dreaming of faithful love. Alena did not want to obey anyone, living by her own rules. With her mother, who abandoned her in her childhood, she often quarreled terribly for any reason, especially because of the tricks of her alcoholic stepfather. He hated Alena, especially after the birth of his own son, and tried his best to oust her from her home.

In the last grade of school, Alena, rather due to pity and curiosity, began dating her lame classmate. Knowing nothing about sex, shortly after prom she discovered her pregnancy. She was only seventeen years old, when under the pressure of public opinion Alena was forced to marry, as they say, "at gunpoint." The family told her that "the child must have an official father" so that she would not be considered "disgraced" in society. But her first marriage was a mistake, and soon turned into many betrayals. This unfortunate marriage exacerbated her already huge problem of trust in people.

After registering the marriage, her young husband Sergey continued to live with his parents, and brought them his salary. Alena with the daughter Lila lived in her mother's house and survived alone as she could. Her husband rarely visited them, did not try to see his daughter or help them with anything. A year later, Sergey's parents sent him to the University of Novosibirsk. Finally, he got his complete freedom; Sergey was happy to live as free as he wanted or was good for him, drank a lot and slept around. Knowing nothing about this, the naive Alena made attempts to "save the family". She flew to him several times, tried to adapt to the fierce cold of the Siberian town. She suffered for a long time the bullying of her drug addict husband, and did not have any chance or money to get out of there, or somehow ending her too early, difficult marriage. Only two years later, having sold all her personal belongings, she returned to Gelendzhik. The first marriage of Alena, as one would expect, was a mistake, and soon turned into a lot of betrayals. This miserable marriage exacerbated her already huge problem of trust in men.

***

In the summer of 1974 Sergey came to Gelendzhik for a vacation. He visited Alena's house and had a fight with her uncle. Outraged Alena wanted to avenge her crippled husband. She wrote an insulting letter to the work of her relative in Moscow. Her uncle's career was in jeopardy, and he started a trial against Alena. But Alena did not expect that her uncle would take her to a court to restore his reputation. At that time, she was quarreling with her relatives, and moved with her daughter to live in a three-room apartment of her mother-in-law. But her mother-in-law was not happy with new tenants, and turned Alena's life into another nightmare.

Alena tried to continue her education at the Krasnodar University, and soon needed to go there for exams. Then, she thought that maybe her first husband would like to restore their marriage. So, she bought tickets to go to him in Novosibirsk again. One morning, Alena took her daughter to a kindergarten, and then went to her work. She told her boss, that she will quit the job, and needed to get her money. But suddenly three men in black suits silently approached her. They took her by the arms, put her in a car, and took her to prison.

Alena begged to give her the opportunity to call home and bring her more comfortable clothes. And most importantly, she needed to get her daughter from the kindergarten. Only at the end of the day, finally, the police on duty, taking pity on her pleas and looking around the empty corridor, gave her the phone. Sergey's mother was not distinguished by sensitivity or kindness. Stubborn mother-in-law could not understand anything from Alena's confused explanation. She began to yell at the frustrated girl, saying that she could not leave work ahead of time. Finally, the mother-in-law agreed to pick up the granddaughter Lila from the kindergarten. But instead of taking the child home to feed and comfort her, Alena's mother-in-law dragged the tired and scared girl to the prison. Alena's daughter saw the mother in the window, was eager to get to her, and began to scream. But the guards did not allow Alena meet her two-year-old child or to explain her that she is not coming home. The mother-in-law with force dragged Lila away holding her hand, not even trying to calm and comfort her. Instead, looking at Alena, mother-in-law was simply annoyed and shouting angrily: *"What will I do with your child? I have to work!"* Despite the recent new quarrel with her own mother, Alena knew that she really loved her granddaughter. Then in despair, she called out to her mother-in-law: *"Take my daughter to my mother."* This heartbreaking scene forever cut into the memory of Alena, tormenting her with a feeling of constant guilt. Lila also remembered it forever.

***

Only at the end of the day a rather young, assertive and very rude investigator Nosova came to prison. In an objectionable tone, the investigator began to ask Alena insulting questions. With condemnation, she began to claim that Alena tried to hide from justice and did not appear for interrogations on many calls. Alena, with tears in her eyes, made excuses, saying that she really did not know anything about the summons for interrogation. She tried to explain that she had long moved to live in another place, then went to the university in the other city, then spent almost a month in the hospital. But the tough investigator did not believe her. Alena really did not understanding why she was arrested. She only repeated that she was not going to hide from anyone. In the end, she was told that she was charged under Article 138 for the defamation. At that moment of cruel and baseless accusation, she felt hopeless despair. The bitter, deep loneliness again swept the soul of the tormented girl. And she just cried out childishly, not knowing that everything was just beginning.

It turned out that at the request of her high-ranking uncle, her family decided to support his lawsuit in order to punish Alena for the insulting letter. Moreover, at the request of her own relatives, it was decided to check the girl with a forensic psychiatrist for sanity. To do this, they planned to send her, like any criminal to the Krasnodar prison. She had to stay in that horrible cell, and wait when enough criminals would be gathered from all over the district to form a train.

After a hysterically-nagging meeting with her little daughter, Alena was taken to a gloomy, damp and cold cell. This dark, windowless, with blank walls cement cell was about 6 x 3 meters in size. One of the ice walls had a small bare and cement elevation for sleeping. In the corner was a stinky barrel (bucket) for the toilet. It was necessary to manage to do everything into it by somehow sitting on a high dirty edge, without falling into the barrel. In the morning, the prisoners rolled out these barrels to empty them.

At that time there, one of the guards was Alena's classmate - Sasha Varchenko. It turned out to be a huge shock for him to suddenly see a "star of his class" locked up as a banal crime in a dirty cold cell. For Alena, it was a shameful, but still comforting luck. She immediately asked him first to send the library textbooks that were with her during the arrest, and return them to the university. She also explained that she had recently been in the hospital, and still had a fever. She asked her classmate to bring her something warm, bypassing all their prison rules. She needed to hide from the cold and damp of that cell. To her surprise, he, a kind soul, did all this, but said that in the morning his shift would end and the other guards would take it all away.

After some time, the guards put another woman to the same cell with Alena. That woman suddenly jumped like a crazy on Alena back and grabbed her hair. Alena began to scream wildly. Security came running, and this crazy woman was taken away. And a day later, a young and very frightened girl Tanya appeared there. She was arrested almost naked right on the beach. When she abandoned her fleeting lover, he stated that she had robbed him. And in order to take revenge on her, he attracted his local friends to this, as his "witnesses."

Tatyana was all shaking from the cold and horror of her hopeless situation. She was threatened with two years in prison under Article No. 144 for the robbery. In order to at least somehow console her, Alena gave her thin blanket, which had been brought the day before by her former classmate. Suddenly, at night, strange sounds began to be heard from a neighboring chamber. Tanya took an iron mug that was given with the tea the day before, put an ear to it, and began to listen. Then, to Alena's great surprise, in response, she too began to gently tap something with the spoon left after a meager dinner.

In a nearby cell two local young men, repeat thieves, sat, waiting for a transfer, as well. Under the ceiling of Alena's cell, there was a small hole. Soon, they began to quickly disassemble it. Late at night, the hole was large enough. Then one of the guys, smiling broadly and gleaming with a mouthful of golden teeth, climbed into the girls' cell. His partner, too, was already half in the same hole, hanging down. But then suddenly a night detour began. Guards saw him, pulled out and started to beat. His heavy moans rolled throughout the prison. And Tanya, hiding in a corner, whispered: *"Now they will come for us, and they will also beat us."*

There was so much fear on her face that she almost turned gray and began to lose consciousness. Alena still twisted in her own beautiful world, considering herself not guilty of anything. She, even in prison, continued to live in the bright illusions and ignorance about real life. Despite her sad situation, Alena still strangely believed in the goodness and justice of the world. She sacredly believed in her guiding star and guardian angel. She could not imagine such atrocities as the beating of women in prison, she could not believe in such cruelty towards her, the beautiful queen of the Greek tribes of Gelendzhik. This time, the girls were lucky. The guards did not come for them. Nothing physical was done for the pacification of the two fools who were flirting with bandits even in the bullpen.

***

Only two weeks later, a special train was assembled to deliver avid criminals to be taken to a regional prison. There were so many women in the cramped car behind bars that not only was there nowhere to sit, but even movement was difficult. Women spent the entire long, eight-hour journey standing. In order to go to the toilet, which located at the end of the car, women had to beg the guard for a long time. Women with shame, a mournful voice, humiliatingly asked him about this vital necessity. The most proud of them endured for as long as they could. There were those who, in spite of everyone, just did all they needed right on the floor of the car. Upon arrival at the Krasnodar Regional Prison, all those arrested were taken to the courtyard, and their names with numbers of articles were read out. Some prisoners reacted to Alena's article 138 with the surprise and curiosity. But others hastily gasped, when someone exclaimed: "*That is the political one!*" After the roll call of each arrested, they asked everyone to strip naked. The women-guards rewrote everything that every person had, put their belongings in a bag, and send it to the storage until the day of the release. Then, they began a humiliating search of the bodies. Overseers in gloves, brazenly and without shame, touched the women in all intimate places, forcing them to bend down. Instead of civilian clothes, they were all given the same prison clothes (bathrobe and shawl). The prisoners received a mattress, a metal mug and a spoon. And then, everyone was sent to a common cell, where there were already more than thirty women.

Entering a huge cell with windows under the ceiling, Alena in fear stopped at the door, listening to the energy of noise, looking around for a quiet place. But several women surrounded her and began to ask why she got into these troubles. Confused Alena did not answer all this turmoil. Her beautiful face looked lost, and her huge brown eyes glowed with grief. Moreover, she didn't know exactly what article No. 138 was about. So, she only nodded in response to the prisoners 'guesses. Two elderly women, ousting everyone else, took Alena to the center of the room, and indicated her place for the night. It was the second tier of the bunk bed, on the metal mesh of which they helped Alena to throw her heavy mattress.

Soon, well and cleanly dressed, beautiful Alena became a prison legend, with special ghosts and inviolability. It was another good luck. For some reason, two elderly prisoners clearly patronized her, protecting from all sorts of duties, usually imposed on new ones. But the very situation and the existence of Alena in a noisy cell, with screams, swearing and fights of inveterate criminals, were terrible for her. In order, that the prisoners would not "stretch" their legs ahead of time, for the whole day they got half a loaf of stale, black bread, one herring and liquid porridge. The food was so scarce that the always graceful Alena lost weight quickly and dangerously. As her grandmother would say, she became just "skin and bones".

One could only dream of silence, peace or solitude there. The most annoying thing was the inability to occupy oneself with something. Everything was forbidden: books, newspapers, any correspondence with the outside world, any communication or meetings. This was a special punishment for everyone under investigation. But even in the complete isolation of a formidable prison, the wildest prisoners still managed to keep secret correspondence with the other prisoners. They did this with the help of ropes and window leaves, even somehow communicating with those who were outside the prison, receiving information and advice on what and how to say during interrogations.

Everyone was taken out for walks twice a week. When the women were taken outside, the guards began search the cells. Each cell was carefully examined and turned upside down. Before that, the guard in a rude voice ordered the prisoners to turn to the wall and hold their hands behind their backs. Alena was not used to obeying rude shouts, and this procedure seemed terribly humiliating to her. So, along the way, walking along the corridor, she gradually dropped her hands. And for some reason, the guards did not even pull her for it, as if realizing that she was not like everyone else. The yard for walks was small, with a closed, high, dull concrete fence, and barbed wire at the top. There were special observation towers at the top of the walls, and armed guards walked around, just like in a movie. In this empty courtyard, in a circle, without stopping or talking, the arrested were supposed to walk. Walking was at least some kind of entertainment. Alena was glad to breathe fresh air, to be in silence, to see the blue sky and rare birds having fun in the wild.

***

Complain

One week later, a medical commission arrived at the prison, and Alena was summoned for examination. After asking a few simple questions, and not finding a mental disorder, they diagnosed "healthy." Then another week passed, but everything was unchanged. Alena began to think that her cruel imprison without a trial has been going on for ages. This prison was in a big, unfamiliar city, where there were neither her friends nor a lawyer. Alena did not have any meetings with her relatives, and there were no additional transfers of food so necessary in the prison. It seemed that everyone had forgotten about her, and the other life that she had before did not exist at all.

But "on the day of complaints" the guards put several pieces of paper and he pencils into the cell. But only few women prisoners interested in them, not believing in success. Alena felt deeply and unjustly punished, and she had nothing to lose. In addition, to her natural optimism, living since childhood in an eternal struggle, Alena was accustomed to use every little chance to improve her life. *"What if something good comes out of my complaint and somebody helps me,"* she thought. She decided to describe her terrible story and the ill-treatment she faced.

By some miracle, this letter was handed over to the chief prosecutor of the Krasnodar. He was very surprised at such a strange incident with an intelligent girl. Apparently, having decided that the Gelendzhik bureaucrats had exceeded their authority, he ordered to improve Alena's conditions in his prison, and send her as soon as possible back to Gelendzhik. The authorities of the regional prison were worried by the intervention of the prosecutor. Soon Alena was transferred to a very small, but quiet, cell for six people.

***

In this new cell for the "intelligentsia," special women, whom they called "millionaires", were sitting under investigation. As it became clear from their conversations, they once worked in the privileged, "Resort Torg", corrupted, and controlled, by a local mafia. There, Alena's mother and her aunt worked, as well. But these arrested prisoners were accused of embezzlement of huge sums of money, of fraud with food and of speculation. In addition the most terrible thing for them was that they were accused of bribery, as well as in the "theft of Soviet property" on an especially large scale.

The investigation had been going on for several years. All this time they were sitting in a tight cell, without the right to see someone, receive newspaper, or any letters. They were like "privileged" prisoners, because they had great connections to the very high people outside. Even some high ranks in Moscow were connected to them and their crime. These ties went to the very top of society, and maybe government. And no one knew how all this could turn out. Therefore, with them, with the "millionaires", everything was very mysterious and difficult. They even went for a walk separately from the rest of the prisoners.

First, they met young Alena coldly, wary, but politely. In this cell, rarely did anyone swear, and there was no negative, frenzied, desperate energy, as there was in the previous big cell. So, it was already a relief for Alena's esthetics. However, at first, the women thought that Alena was planted for them on purpose, that she might be a spy. Therefore, they communicated among themselves in some incomprehensible, conditional language. But Alena did not ask them anything, and did not talk at all, busy with her thoughts. So, they soon relaxed a bit, and generally stopped paying attention to the young cellmate

Once Alena was horrified to see that they were often taken to interrogations. After that they returned, barely dragging their legs, bruised, with battered hair and abrasions. They courted each other sympathetically, slowly coming to a "normal" state, as it were before. And then, at leisure, they played their homemade cards or tell fortunes on cards guessing about the future. They taught Alena how to play the card game "Preference", the main entertainment of the prison.

In this creepy cell, with fat, weak and battered women, Alena became a witness to their difficult life stories. Sharp in her mind and observant, she realized that they were still hoping that they would be rescued by "Iron Bela". They respectfully mentioned the name of Bela, calling her Naumovna. Upon learning that Alena's mother also worked in the "Resort Torg", the prisoners stopped hiding something from the innocent looking Alena. But she did not tell them that this sonorous name of Bela had been familiar to her since childhood. Her mother was friends with the almighty Bela, who handled millions around maybe the whole Soviet Union. Bela even sometimes visited Emma's new home, always bringing something special. She beautifully smiled, amiably talking quietly with her grandmother. After Bela's visits, life in the parental home became calmer and more comfortable.

But, as it turned out later, Bela could not help her former co-workers, prisoned for the crime they committed together. Soon, she was also arrested and brutally tortured. "High posts" made Bela a "scapegoat", cleaning, sweeping their own criminal traces, hiding their own crimes. She was shot in 1982, having survived Alena's mother for only three years.

***

Punishment

Alena spent a hard month in a Soviet investigative prison. She saw there too much bad stuff and heard all that usually happens in such places. Having been released, she never told anyone about what was happening there, in a terrible place of congestion. Sometimes she met there the innocent victims of the Soviet regime and pressure machine. Once in Gelendzik someone gave her Solzhenitsyn's book, *"One Day of Ivan Denisovich"*, which was banned in the Soviet Union. This small work of a banned immigrant described very accurately what Alena herself personally experienced in the prison. But the guardian angel hovered over Alena, and her "miracles in the sieve" continued. Apparently thanks to the written complaint, Alena was soon returned to Gelendzhik. She gave a recognizance not to leave, and was left alone before the trial. At her mother's house she found her little daughter Lila, who also needed love and care. Lila was insanely happy to see her mother. And only in the tender affection of her daughter, Alena drew her strength to continue her life. Right after her arrest, Alena was fired from her previous job at the Research Institute of Sea Geophysics. In the small town, where everyone knew each other, it was very difficult to find any job. But Alena, overcoming depression, began to prepare for her defense in the court.

At this time, her first husband, Sergei, was still in Novosibirsk. He did not know anything about the sad situation of his former classmate and the mother of his daughter. His parents did not tell him anything, "for his own good," as his mother said. But when on the day of his birth on October 28 he did not receive the expected congratulatory telegram from Alena, Sergei called his parents and asked about her. And only then they reported what had happened to his wife. Soon, he flew to Gelendzhik and began to collect the money for Alena's very expensive lawyer.

The moral-indicative court was prepared quickly. Sudden imprisonment, heinous examination in the neuropsychiatric dispensary, all was organized by relatives as a punishment for Alena. Now, the main thing for her uncle, who started this, was that, she had to be formally convicted and be punished. With her conviction, he planned to be rehabilitated at his work. And his career, damaged by her insulting letter, could somehow recover.

All Gelendzhik relatives came to court, except for the relatives of her husband. Alena stood in the courtroom, surrounded by a condemning crowd, not seeing any protection or salvation. Only once did she turn back and look at her mother, who was sitting with her eyes downcast. Then she looked at her beloved grandmother with bitter pursed lips, and at the grinning stepfather. All of them participated in this conspiracy, in this performance. In the testimony, the stepfather tried the most. He struggled to look for unfavorable examples from her past, trying to prove that she was always a problem child. Alena, looking at her "family", could not believe that her seemingly close people demanded for her a terrible punishment. All her many years of illusions, the expectations of their understanding and love, everything was destroyed.

A terrible fire of revenge flared up in Alena's soul. She could no longer forgive her relatives for all the cruelty with which they had treated her all her twenty years. They crossed the line of no return, and Alena's heart almost did not feel any love for them. For a moment, her eyes flashed with a terrible fire of despair. Then, the incredible stream of a strange energy of destruction flew from her eyes towards her relatives. But it was too late to regret about anything.

The lawyer Bogdan faithfully worked for the entire amount paid to her. From a variety of people, she collected a lot of positive reviews about Alena. To them she attached numerous diplomas and letters of commendation, which the girl received annually from various public organizations for her activity. Friends and several scientific leaders from her previous job (where everybody loved Alena) came to this court hearing. They spoke highly of the girl's personality and her diligent work. All that she was accused of sounded ridiculous, and did not fit with the beautiful appearance of an intelligent beauty. Then, in order to make a more negative impression on the judge, the prosecutor began to read offensive quotes from the letter that Alena had sent her uncle to work. Despite the truthfulness of the facts, the rudeness of the expressions and the emotional coloring with which the letter was read out loud, they did not fit the appearance of a fragile girl. Everything sounded very unsightly. Alena's face was burning with shame, and she quietly cried from this public humiliation. One of her former and brave colleague rose from his seat. He said loudly, that even the most insulting letter with half the truth that sounded here, was still not such a big crime for which you could just grab a man on the street and send him to prison. But he was immediately and sharply stopped. His ardent, protective speech was immediately and rudely interrupted. He got a clear threat, and humbly sat down.

***

In Soviet times, a passport and a "records of work book" were the main documents of any person. By virtue of Russian laws, if a person was under investigation, a court, or a condemning a sentence, all of it led to a shameful stamp and a record in a special "records of work book". The fatal record of one of the event in the "record of work book" was the worst punishment. It was for a lifetime. In that heyday of "communist stagnation" with such a record, a person was forever marked with a black, indelible stain. He could never get a good job. Learning about it too late, Alena's mother dragged her to the police chief to ask him not to make such a terrible record, not to break the fate of a young girl. Everyone in the city knew and respected Emma. She was always kind and responsive to all, and helped many with scarce goods. In addition, she was a friend of the famous

"Iron Bela", with whom she worked together. Everyone tried to please "Iron Bela" and her friends.

At that time, universal mutual responsibility, a bribe was in the order of things, and it was used to achieve success in any business. It all depended only on the purpose and size of the bribe. This visit to the chief of police was no exception, because fate of the daughter was at stake. So mother Emma presented the chief of police with imported warm leather gloves. At that time, in a country of continuous deficit, this was a generous gift. Gloves like this were impossible to find anywhere. Then, they simply and unconcernedly talked about this and that. The police chief smiled happily from his unlimited power. Alena sat nearby, burning with shame. But the fateful record was not made.

In Alena's tormented soul, no one could erase the horror that she experienced in all these trials. An indelible mark of family betrayal and an abusive court forever remained in her soul a bleeding wound. Many painful years of suffering and bitter wanderings have passed. Forgiveness in Alena's soul was finally found, but by this time there was no one on earth to whom she could give it.

***

After the trial, Alena was must to find a job in order to fulfil the punishment was awarded to her, and pay a huge fine to the state. To Alena's surprise, her mother-in-law helped her. Without telling anyone about Alena's conviction, she got her a job at the Sanatorium-Forest School, where she herself worked for many years. Knowing nothing about Alena's past and having no criminal record in her "record of work book", she was assigned to work as a copy machine operator.

These huge machines stood in a special room without windows. The room had a heavy metal door, which Alena always locked with a key. Next to it was another office where Alena received visitors with the job orders. In fact, there was little work and the school teachers only occasionally brought her various documents for copying. To reproduce or print copies, they brought written permission from the director of the institution. However, hazardous chemicals were used to work with these copy machines. Therefore, after work, these two rooms, for which Alena was responsible, had to be well ventilated with through air.

For this position Alena received a minimum wage of that time, only seventy rubles. In addition, accounting office took a large portion of Alena's salary to give it to the State. For her life Alena got a very small amount of money, which was even lower than the official living wage. Alena had to live on it together with her daughter.

It is interesting to recall that in Soviet times, dissidents used every opportunity to print forbidden literature somewhere. Then, "self-published" anti-Soviet material was very popular, and some people did it by reprinting banned authors. Ironically, the former 'prisoner' Alena was arranged to work in this secret office of photocopiers. Soon after, a court order for a fine arrived to her new job place. That information from the accounting office spread on gossips and rumors. Despite the fact that Alena did not have a message about the prison and court in her "record of the work book', everyone soon found out about her "criminal" experience. But they had no right to dismiss her from the job under government requirements and conditions of the court.

During the day it was boring to sit in the enclosed rooms. So, Alena rented a tape recorder from the secretary of the organization, and enjoyed the scandalous political, sharp songs of the popular singer Vladimir Vysotsky. Thinking that the walls of her office were rather thick, she turned on the tape recorder quite loudly. From her secret cabinet, the anti- soviet songs sounded very defiant.

Ironically, in the same small corridor where the copy rooms were, cleaner worker lived. She often was drunk, asked Alena to loan her some money, and hated that Alena never gave her any. Once, having gone home, Alena forgot to close the window in her "secret room". Strangely during the same night somebody got into her office and stole the tape recorder.

In the morning, in a fright, Alena immediately announced about it to the administration. But no one believed her because she was "previously convicted". They immediately convened a Komsomol meeting, condemned her, deciding to expel Alena from that communist's organization for young adults. At that time, it was intended to be another humiliating punishment. In addition, the administration decreed an additional deduction from her salary to cover the cost of the lost tape recorder. Someone superbly warmed up on the naivety or negligence of Alena.

***

For almost a year Alena was forced to continue to live and work in Gelendzhik. She dreamed of a time when she could leave behind all this bedlam and disappear from that hostile town forever. But this was not the whole bitter cup that she was to drink. In Gelendzik rumors spread fast, overgrown with all sorts of absurdities. People said, "if there was a court and a verdict, it means she was guilty", and many people tried to avoid Alena.

But once, one hairdresser, admiring Alena's chic hair, invited her to participate in a regional hairstyle contest. Alena was invited to such competitions before, even in Novosibirsk, where she lived for several years with her first husband. In Alena's sad life, especially after all the previous troubles, such invitation was a huge event. And she happily agreed. Leaving for the whole day of the competition in the neighboring city of Novorossiysk, Alena took with her a red, leather bag, where she put her things. When everyone changed clothes for the performance, Alena did not notice that her neighbor also had a similar red bag, almost the same as hers. But Alena was pure and naive, and did not attach any importance to this. The competition was especially fun, noisy and beautiful. Alena was very proud that her master hairdresser with her help took second place in the region. Alena joyfully demonstrated her fashionable hairstyle and the skills of her hairdresser, walking on the red carpet under the sounds of the hall buzzing with delight. At night they returned to Gelendzhik.

A week after this trip, one evening, a group of angry women suddenly came into Alena's courtyard. They unceremoniously broke into Alena's house, waking her relatives and demanding the return of someone else's red bag. They cursed and poured mud on her, accusing her of stealing. They recalled that it was she who had already been convicted before this contest. Shocked Alena, panting from the resentment, showed them her own red bag, assuring that she could not take someone else's. But the women left as angry as they came, dissatisfied, not believing in Alena's explanations. After a while, notorious bag was found. But no one apologized to Alena. She felt that no matter what, she would never be able restore her good name in this town.

After the trial, it became completely unthinkable to live in her mother's house, as well. The stepfather continued to openly mock Alena, especially when no one was home. Once she could not stand his insults anymore. When he turned to the refrigerator, she hit him with a knife. But a short and sharp blade of a knife popped into her palm, deeply cutting her fingers. Mother called 911, Alena was taken to the hospital, and a doctor sewed up her wounds. But after the plaster cast was removed, Alena discovered that the inept doctor could not connect the tendons correctly. So, Alena's two fingers could no longer fully extend. She could not anymore play the piano, in which previously she had been fond of and found solace and oblivion from troubles. Together with the breasts extended after the childbirth, twisted fingers even more strengthened her sense of inferiority and insecurity. She struggled with it for a long time, but solved these problems much later by doing plastic surgery.

Alena's hard-working mother loved her granddaughter Lila and took care of her, as best she could. After the case with the knife, the stepfather continued to drink for weeks, slept with other women, and brought Emma pain and illness. No matter what, it all came down to one conclusion: Alena had to leave home once and for all. And mother said to Alena's face, that she could not live in this house. Needing money, Alena began selling furniture and carpets from her part of the parental home. Her mother, with a face dark from grief, stood at the window. She looked at things disappearing from her house but, for some reason, did not stop her daughter, wounded from childhood. Having finally completed the Gelendzhik period, in desperation Alena flew with her daughter again to her first husband in Novosibirsk. It was her bitter, repeated mistake. There she was stuck in poverty, cold and hunger for another two years. But then, with the great effort, she was able to get to Leningrad.

While Alena's mother was alive she gathered whole family around her. Every year, all her relatives from all over Russia were attracted by Emma's smiling, generous character and hospitality and visited her house on the warm Black Sea. But she was terminally ill for more than ten years, and partial operations did not help. After her terrible death, her mother Anna tried to gather all relatives nearby, continuing to bind them into a single whole. But when she was gone, everything fell into pieces, which there was no one else to collect.

***

Seagull

An elegant and very young girl stands at the stern of a small boat and feeds the seagulls. She has a classic Greek profile, giving her face an exquisite uniqueness. A black, wet swimsuit almost completely envelops her flexible, snake-like body. That swimming suit, like the skin of a dolphin, perfectly outlines its soft, classic contours. The sun caresses her tanned skin, slightly covered with small, white spots of salt from a recent swim in the sea. A light, warm wind plays with her long, brown hair. Her beautiful curls drift lushly on the shoulders, flow in the wind like wings.

A passenger boat rushes along the Black Sea, forming behind a white foam of waves. Sea gulls circle around the ship. They pick up pieces of bread on the fly, which are thrown to them by the young beauty. And the girl thinks that she is one of these gulls, and has fun spinning with her friends. She, too, is absolutely free, and soars easily on her wide-spread wings. When she gets tired, she can simply lie down on a fresh, elastic stream of sea air and relax. And the wind will just carry her behind the ship. More than anything, she adores her bewitching freedom, this salty, caressing wind and the shining sea.

Here she looks around the vast expanse of the sea. From above everything is clearly visible to the horizon. And she can see deep down as well, almost to the bottom, where there are a lot of different tasty fish. Watching the fish below underwater is also exciting and enjoyable. The girl is embraced by inner joy from the feeling of extraordinary freedom and the expectation of something magical that is bound to happen. This boundless joy overwhelms her, makes her unusually happy. Her whole soul sings, full of hope and expectation.

The hot blood of her Greek ancestors flows in her, and her whole essence is eager to accomplish something extraordinary. She looks at the blinding sun and cries from her overwhelming feelings, from the sensation of this unforgettable moment, which will never happen again.

On this beautiful, hot, summer day, she recalls her favorite book, "*Jonathan Livingston Seagull*".

She cries from her unbridled thirst for freedom. She cries about her beautiful, so innocent and young life, flying so quickly over the horizon

***

Leningrad

Alena went to live in Leningrad, dreaming of a beautiful and more intellectual life in the northern capital. But to stay more than one month in this stunning city was only possible with official registration at the police office. The path to this was only through marriage, and Alena began looking for a suitable person. Soon, she met a thirty-three-year-old Jew named Sergei Berz, same as her first husband. Sergey was never married, lived comfortably with his mother, and worked as a theater director. *"That chance could be successful"*, thought Alena, and did her best to charm him to accelerating her marriage. But his habit of freedom did not harmonize with Alena's ideas about devotion and fidelity. Moreover, as Alena quickly learned, his imperious mother, who loved to control everything around her, supported the free life of her son, indulging his whims. In everything, Alena depended on their quirks, and had to put up and adapt to their rules and way of life.

The vulnerable girl, who had already lived a hard life, needed love and tenderness and could not abide new humiliation. In addition, the independent character of Alena (Aquarius) did not endure any restrictions. The proud temper of a Greek woman, who grew up in complete freedom, did not allow her to be comfortable with the role of a maid or just a housekeeper. One year in the tiny apartment was full of differences, struggles, and effort to get rid of Alena and her little daughter. Then, her second husband and his mother realized that they couldn't just simply push and throw Alena back to Gelendzhik. Unable to get rid of her, the second Sergey filed for divorce. However, according to the law and the court order, they were forced to provide Alena with her small daughter a good size room. So, finally, Alena got her own living space in the city of her dreams.

***

Artist Valery

Shortly after the second divorce, once at the Hermitage, Alena met a surprisingly attractive guy with huge, burning eyes and long hair, hair to the shoulders. This handsome man turned out to be a very talented artist named Valery. He had just arrived in Leningrad from Ukraine, and enrolled in a restoration school. Apparently, he also dreamed of registering in this city.

This time Alena was lucky to meet a very good, kind and pleasant man. They both were only twenty-five years old, and Alena was his first woman. Most importantly, he was an interesting conversationalist and Alena enjoyed listening and talking to him. At that time, as always, Alena worked a lot and needed some help. Valery happily spent time with her eight-year-old daughter, took Lila from school and helped her to do homework. Soon Valery became a simply irreplaceable friend, and they got married.

Alena and Valery lived happy together for ten years. But, despite his calmness and kindness, Alena often could not rely on him. Valera was in the habit of promising something, but not fulfilling his promises. Looking into his beautiful black eyes, Alena tried to trust him, but all his promises turned out to be lies. He always had in mind to do good things, but he just could not accomplish what he promised. In addition, he did not want to officially work anywhere, explaining that his desire was to paint pictures and be just an artist.

Finally, Alena arranged for him to work at the school, where her daughter was studying. But soon after, he began to date an English teacher there. For little Lila, the betrayal of the man whom she considered her "father" was a great grief. Alena also could never forgive anyone for the broken promises to be faithful. One day, her eyes were opened to her husband's infidelity. Then, she managed to immediately unregister him out of her wonderful apartment and changed the locks. Valery was too slow, and first did not want to fight nor try to exchange an apartment. He did not have the courage or strength to use the law in order to get a room or his share through the court. Knowing Alena's strong character he did not want to fight at all with her. He simply moved to his friend, taking with them their dog Brake and their cat Tosha. When he began to fight for his room, it was too late. Alena had already sold that apartment.

During "perestroika", unable to do anything but painting, Valery could not find employment in Leningrad (St. Petersburg). He did not know where to apply himself or how to make money. Several times he borrowed money from Alena, but did not repay it. And then she, out of old friendship, and feeling sorry for Valery, tried to help him, giving him work as her driver. But, not accustomed to work somewhere regularly, Valery did not like it, and soon quit this job.

In the end, Valery was completely disappointed in the circumstances of his collapsed life in St. Petersburg. He abandoned his dog Brake to his friend, and the dog soon died, unable to bear separation from his former beloved family. And Valery, grabbing his cherished cat, went to his homeland to live in his mother's house. Finally, there he was able to find his way, painting the walls and creating the icons of the local cathedral. Alena later, already living in America, the country of her dreams, wrote a book about her youth, Russian life, and about Valery's early, Leningrad work.

***

Crossroads

Russian communist propaganda has generated many negative stereotypes about capitalist countries. In the 1960s and 1970s, English and military training were compulsory subjects in schools. On the radio and in newspapers they constantly talked about the threat of war with the United States. For almost seventy years, Russian citizens lived under the invisible "Iron Curtain," with virtually no opportunity to travel abroad. Only Russian Jews could obtain permission to immigrate to Israel. Many beautiful stereotypes were created about the unattainable and wonderful life abroad. Some who went abroad on business trips, seafarers, and their wives created these tales. Greatly exaggerated, almost fantastic tales of a beautiful and prosperous life abroad grew everywhere. And then, they were also enhanced by Hollywood films. Especially the country of paradise - USA, inaccessible to most Russian people, was praised the most. Like many others, Alena grew up in Russia with the thought that America is the only place where everyone wants to immigrate.

During the communist time, getting to know foreigners was undesirable and suspect. This was regarded as treason and betrayal of the homeland. Women who met with foreigners were monitored and severely punished. They were most often forced to "work" for the State Security Committee, and report to the KGB details of their exchanges and conversations with foreigners. Alena was not from a Jewish family who would be allowed to emigrate. For all non-Jews, there was only one legal way to leave the country: to marry a foreigner. However, Alena was fed up with her previous forced marriages, and had no good reason to do it. The very thought of marriage was disgusting to her.

In the early 1990s, Russia began an extraordinary, dramatic transformation initiated by President Mikhail Gorbachev. After the failed coup of the Communists, supporters of Yeltsin's hard line, a disastrous decision was made to dissolve the Soviet Union. Many described the situation in Russia at that time as a "tragedy of historical proportions." In fact, in the 1990s the economic situation in Russia worsened. People who worked hard still did not receive a salary of more than forty dollars a month.

At this time, Alena lost her favorite work as a museum guide. Nevertheless, she was more fortunate than most people because she had many true friends and excellent connections. But most importantly, she was very hardworking and optimistic. One day, one of her enterprising friends invited her to join their new pharmaceutical business. There has always been a shortage of medical drugs in Russia, and such a business promised to be very profitable. Therefore, Alena did not think too long and grabbed luck by the tail. She boldly invested most of her savings in this new business, and devoted all her time to the new work.

Life tempered the character of Alena. But her appearance still retained the features of a holy, pure Madonna. In 1995, she was almost forty, but she underwent plastic surgery and looked very young. In addition, her many friends and fans considered her a smart, well-read, highly educated and successful business woman. That's improved her self-esteem. Despite the fact that she already seemed to have lived a long life, her soul was still young, full of hope and kept the thirst for life.

During the "perestroika" Alena felt that she had finally achieved everything that seemed to be possible for an enterprising woman in Russia. By this time, she had a high income, she was provided with everything, and did not depend on anyone. She became an independent business lady. Thanks to her energy and desire to overcome all obstacles, her business quickly began to gain momentum. Soon a dizzying success came to her, and Alena firmly stood on her feet. By the mid-1990s, she was already able to buy two cars, as well as a second apartment for her daughter in the same building where she lived. Moreover, when most people only dreamed of having a vacation on the sea at least once in their life, Alena several times a year took her family to Italy, Malta and Greece.

Soon in Greece her daughter met a young guy, who not only was dating Lila, but also was interested in selling his fur coats in the big cities of Russia. Lila began to do it with him. The money she earned gave her an excellent life for some time. It is also took a burden off Alena's shoulders, for she had supported her daughter and granddaughter all her life. However, soon uncontrolled gangsters put the entire small business in Russia at risk. In St. Petersburg, it was dangerous to store valuables in your home. Once, Lila's apartment with several fur coats was looted.

In order to survive this dangerous time, Alena tried to work as quietly as possible, trying to hide her profitable business from racketeers and gangsters. She brought her scarce medical goods for sale only to some of the surviving factories, which people could access only by special pass. There, under the protection of police guarding the entrance, she worked in the lobby having her temporary mobile kiosk. But this did not last long. The field of activity narrowed, fear grew, and business suffered losses. Several times Alena's elderly, loyal driver and the bodyguard were caught and beaten and the money was stolen. After that, they left the job, leaving Alena alone. It was difficult for her to find a new driver or new places where would it be easy and safe to sell the medicine. Her savings were getting low.

With each new day, it became increasingly difficult for her to live alone, supporting a comfortable lifestyle, which she greatly valued. But if she stopped earning every day, then all her savings would disappear very quickly. And in St. Petersburg there was still the same cold climate, slush, endless rains, gloomy skies, dirty streets and empty shops. No money could compensate for the unpleasant social conditions and unsightly habitat.

Of course, Alena could still go to live in her Gelendzhik, where she grew up. The resort town was especially pleasant from April to October. The warm gentle sea and the sun always quickly restored Alena's strength, removing any spiritual burden. But in a small town there was practically no work. In the most beautiful city of her childhood, with amazing nature and climate, there were too many bitter memories. Only the graves of her relatives awaited her there. Alena could not even walk the streets without pain and tears.

Then Alena thought even more deeply about where to arrange her life more comfortably and more stably.

Having lived a life very full of emotions, events and work, Alena was sure that she deserved more than she had in Russia. She traveled a lot and was a "citizen of the world". As a result, she thought she had experienced and known life in foreign countries. She was confident in herself, believing that she could easily live in any place, and that she would not have difficulties with adaptation anywhere. She did not realize at that time that being a tourist and living constantly in an unfamiliar country are two different things.

At the same time, unscrupulous deceivers who succeeded in all kinds of frauds thrived in Russia. It became especially popular to open marriage dating agencies. There, trusting Russian women, for high fees, were offered "quickly and safely" to marry a foreigner for improving their lives.

Leningrad (Saint Petersburg) has always been a city of tourists. After the "perestroika", there were especially many foreign tourists, and the opportunity to communicate with them became much more accessible. In addition, Alena was a guide, and constantly working with people; she had the skills of easy communication with any person. Being a curious and venturesome person, she decided to study foreign candidates for husbands. In this period of her prosperous life, Alena did not have to marry under duress, as before. She did not need to marry in order to better arrange her life, give birth to a child or obtain a residence permit in a big city. A new, completely exciting time has come for her. She no longer needed a man to help her, or to use him as an elevator to move on to a higher quality of life. And this was a relief. It seemed that she could freely choose the one she wanted, according to her taste and desire.

However, over time and with the growth of her well-being, the requirements for the spiritual and emotional qualities of men increased. Her plans did not include adjusting to the lower spiritual level of a man. Her man needed to be a smart and attractive person, not a cheater or a shriveled freak. Moreover, Alena had no desire to move to the apartment of a man who lived with his mother, or to share with him her own apartment. She could not imagine life with an old or constantly grumbling man, especially if he made less money than she.

Now, Alena, with her deep emotionality, originality, expressive soul, and with her exceptional requirements for a man, it has become even more difficult to get along with anyone else. It has become even more difficult for her to find a good guy with whom it would be interesting spend time together, who would satisfy her spiritual and emotional essence, without constantly demanding sex. Alena understood that only compromises make a marriage truly happy. But she could not decide which of the above she could sacrifice for a new marriage.

As often happens, successful and attractive women of forty years old liked younger men. But Alena often met gigolos or controlling despots. At parties where Alena was often invited, around the graceful, elegant and smart woman the successful "new" Russians circled. They got rich in the wake of "perestroika," and not always in a legitimate or pure way. These young guys were often spoiled upstarts, without education, good manners, or simply arrogant bandits, without morality and principles. Money for them had the main value, and was the meaning of life. They were not shy in the means for their achievement. These categories of men could not be a good choice for partnership or Alena's next marriage.

Alena often met men with wrinkled faces and fatty deposits, who were too much battered by promiscuous partying, excesses, wine and cigarettes. Despite their own problems, they were still looking for a young woman or a woman without children, who would focus all her attention on them. In addition, the elderly Russian men had bad smell. Moreover, they had a very unpleasant habit of pouring their feelings and problems on a woman, using her as a psychotherapist. Alena had enough of her own internal problems and experiences, and was not interested in listening to their constant whining, or their constant digging in their own feelings. It was boring and burdensome. Despite all of the above, Alena was still a romantic person, and dreamed of meeting real, great love. The appearance of new children was excluded for her. She needed a caring person who would be absolutely faithful to her. Alena simply wanted to live easily and joyfully, without domestic or emotional problems, without fear of being deceived or betrayed. At the same time, she did not want to emigrate and depend on anyone in a foreign country.

After carefully considering all the options, she sent her ad to a special magazine where men wanted to find a Russian wife. Thousands of letters came to Alena from different countries. Among them were many tempting offers. Now she just had to choose a prosperous country where she could live without problems and worries.

***

Paris

In general, Russians are very kind, gullible, hospitable and open people. But before the "perestroika" they practically did not go abroad, and least of all knew something about America, except for some stereotypes from the movies. In Russian magazines, American men were portrayed with large cigars. It was said that they do not like to work, but only play golf. Travel circles confirmed that most American tourists were fat, slow, uneducated, and arrogant.

After the "perestroika", many foreign adventurers and elderly lovers of young girls flooded Russia in search of easily accessible, naive women. Alena's friends often warned her that only losers with some sexual, financial, economic or personal problems try to find a lowly bride in third world countries. Such men were confident that a woman from a poor country would be more flexible, accommodating and cheap. They suggested that she would easily put up with all the problems encountered in their countries, would not be demanding or controlling, as their local women were.

Such talk about foreigners looking for cheap brides bothered Alena. When she received letters from candidates for a Russian wife, she tried to find the catch in their letter. Any letter immediately showed the character of their author, and some of the messages seemed pretty smart. Others tried to be even more thoughtful. They put in the envelop one dollar for the postage for the "bride" to reply. It was good, and such letters got initial attention. But first of all, Alena looked through letters with photos, choosing men according to their facial expressions. The face of each person reflects his character and his lifestyle.

There were so many letters that to view all of them took several hours a day. Most letters were written by hand in foreign language. Poor knowledge of English and slow translation with a dictionary took too much time. Some letters had many tempting offers, but it was a laborious process, which took a lot of effort and valuable time. The previous marriages and life experiences taught Alena to not trust the intentions of all these men.

It became apparent that relationships at a distance or through letters are a hopeless illusion that could bring unpleasant surprises. Then, it turned out that the local "Dating Bureau" had long become just pimps earning from the use of gullible women for their own quick enrichment.

In addition, soon the postal office people also realized that there was money in the envelopes. They began to open envelopes, extracting money before delivering letters. Alena did not have time or desire to study long letters from abroad, and became completely uninterested in receiving them.

Gradually, Alena realized that the fears of her friends were correct. And after several real meetings with foreigners, she finally lost all interest in such a process. On her way to a new marriage, there were too many circumstances and conditions that had to be met before she agreed to marry a new man, especially an unknown foreigner.

***

It seemed easiest to go to the capital of France. For everyone who wanted to get out of Russia during all kinds of upheavals, it was France that was the most obvious choice for emigration. Moreover, for several centuries, knowledge of French culture and language was mandatory for the Russian aristocracy and high society.

Paris was very close, in Europe, just two hours from Alena's beloved St. Petersburg. Both cities surprised with their similar architectural ensembles, built by the same architects, in the same style. Paris, like St. Petersburg, was the center of many exciting events, exhibitions and museums, magnificent parks and cultural institutions. Alena's perception of Paris was formed with the help of romantic French literature. She had read a lot, and loved Balzac, Maupassant, Dumas and other French writers. So, after the "perestroika" the first city to travel to was Paris. There she found several families of the old Russian intelligentsia - well-settled and wealthy people. And even she herself began to take private French lessons. There, in her previous trips, Alena had already met several of the applicants for her "hand and heart". It seemed to Alena that France would be her main choice for a future life, and it would be logical to settle there.

Most often, Paris met Alena with a drizzling rain, gray sky and low clouds. The climate there was also almost the same as in St. Petersburg. Alena did not feel "abroad." But when friends began to take her to chic restaurants with extremely high prices, she soon felt that she could not afford it. This lifestyle was not for her. Also, on the streets of Paris, she was not free at all, or incognito, as in St. Petersburg. She could not walk alone or disappear into the crowd, enjoying something, without the intrusive attention of men. One winter, putting on her magnificent mink coat, Alena went for a walk along the Champs Elysees. It stretches from Concorde Square to the Arc de Triumph, about 1915 meters easily walkable. This is a very pleasant place for a walk, with the shining lights of decorated trees, attractive shop windows and cafes. But when Alena got to Concord Square, a car stopped right next to her. An elegantly dressed man, smiling amiably, offered to give her a lift to the hotel. But soon after Alena got in, he turned to the nearest underground parking and began to annoyingly offer to have sex for an impressive fee. It sounded as it was normal for him, as if it was in the order of things. But such a discovery shocked Alena, and she stopped going for walks alone the beautiful streets of Paris.

Soon Alena realized that everything was for sale in the capital of Europe. Fleeting sex was the main motive and stimulus for the life of devastated people. Paris, as it was sung in the famous song, *"day and night, burned in a circular passion, when the fatal force conquered new lips, carrying away the illusion of a beautiful dream."* It was a constant carnival in the late hours of the Paris nights. It seemed that men did not have any significant hobbies, nor exciting work. It seemed that they did not think about anything substantial, did not value anything but good food and sex. Obviously, most of them were bored, had nothing to occupy themselves with, and they were looking for daily adventures. Soon Alena was very tired of the carefree Parisians. She met apparently very superficial, living just one day wealthy and spoiled, but such weak men of Paris.

In her repeated visits to Paris, she was still trying to assess how good French men could be for a stable, lasting relationship and marriage. But time passed without a tangible positive result. And the French were elegant dandies, who loved themselves most of all, and who did not plan "serious intentions".

In addition, the men there competed with each other for a good woman. They drove Alena to the most expensive nightclubs, trying to make the best, as they thought, impression. One day she asked to be taken to theater or opera, to a concert, or to an exhibition. She wanted to go to more interesting and more spiritual places. But in response, she saw only their bewilderment and was very disappointed. It became clear that in Paris it was most likely good to just relax, and a good vacation required a lot of money. But a permanent life in such a carefree atmosphere was not for Alena, and soon she became very bored.

Visa

In Alena's favorite ancient Greek mythology, King Aegeus possessed huge herds. All of them were kept in special stables. For many years, manure was not exported from these stables, so terrible chaos was happening there. In order to clean them, King Aegeus hired Hercules. Hercules in a cunning way diverted water from two rivers there, and these rivers simply washed out all the manure.

After disappointment in the frivolous men of Paris, Alena came to the conclusion that it was time to clean the "Augean Stables". It was time to put things in order at home, in her plans, and in the head. In the mid-1990s, Alena saw that the time had come when it became much easier to overcome the obstacles to obtaining a tourist visa in the United States. Her friends helped her find one person in the government who promised to make such a visa without problems, but for good money.

At that time, the real price of a tourist visa in the United States was about fifty dollars. The average salary of an ordinary Russian person was also about fifty dollars a month. And the recommended official asked to pay him a huge sum of $2,000 for a tourist visa with multiple entries into the United States. Having decided on this, Alena began to raise money by selling all her valuables. She sold the car and gave him the money.

But then another huge problem arose. A similar visa to the USA was issued only if the person had a special return ticket for the plane, although without a return date. It was a very expensive nonrefundable ticket. Alena had no other choice, but to buy such a ticket, having spent another thousand dollars to purchase it.

After that, another problem arose. In fact, Alena did not know anyone in the United States. She had no idea where to go there directly from the airport, or what could be done there at all. After selling a car, an apartment and other valuables, after acquiring an expensive visa and an expensive ticket, she was in a hopeless situation. There was no turning back. Then the average *"Regular Pig Bean"* turned up to her. We will call him just *"Regular Bean"* further on.

***

Copy Rights

Author is Elena Bulat. No part of this publication may be reproduced, distributed, or transmitted in any form or by any means, including photocopying, recording, or other electronic or mechanical methods, without the prior written permission of the publisher, except in the case of brief quotations embodied in critical reviews and certain other noncommercial uses permitted by copyright law. The title of a book printed in the United States of America. The main category of the book is Biography, memorial. Other category is Family, Soviet Union. First Edition was in 2020. Photos and logo done by Elena Bulat.

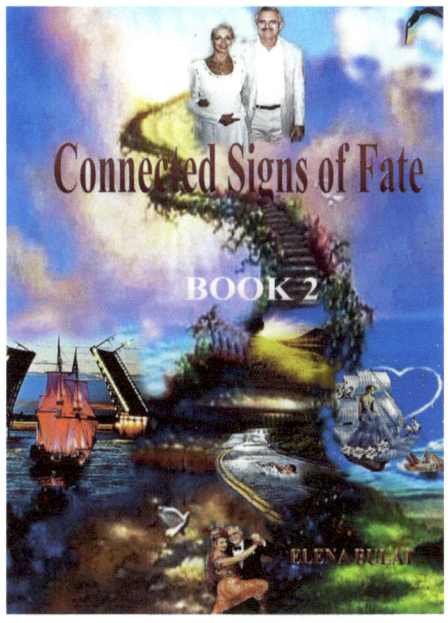

***
AllRightsReserved2021@ElenaPankey

www.ingramcontent.com/pod-product-compliance
Lightning Source LLC
Chambersburg PA
CBHW041950240426
43669CB00044B/41